BONNIE'S
Blessings

BONNIE KLOCKENGA

BONNIE'S BLESSINGS
by Bonnie Klockenga
Copyright © 2023 Bonnie's Blessings

Cover photo: designed in Canva

NOTE TO READER
Disclaimer

Bonnie desires for the reader to know that *Bonnie's Blessings is* a compilation of wisdom that Bonnie has gained through the years from her time in the church, listening to sermons, doing women's bible studies, and reading devotionals.

Bonnie's Blessings is mixture of her own thoughts and all that she has learned over the years from being a faithful and devoted follower of Jesus.

With that being said, it would be impossible to give credit to every person that has impacted her words. She does not take full credit for her words, but wants to acknowledge and say thank you to all of you who through the years have ministered to her in countless ways. May you know the full impact of your actions and be blessed for your fruit. Amen.

Growing up, I was simply "blessed with the best." ··· in this special photo, with our Dad, Joe Seggelke, was taken as we were making preparations go to South Korea as missionaries. He was an amazing Dad and dedicated servant of God. He and Mother taught us about The Lord by their words and their actions. I clearly recall the previous Sunday when my Dad baptized me. And the blessed day he walked me down the aisle to marry my Bud. We were at his bedside with mother when he took his last breath. Every day I think of them both and thank God for such amazing parents.

v.

Bonnie

January

January 1

"Yes, my soul, find rest in God; my hope comes from him. Truly he is my rock and my salvation; he is my fortress, I will not be shaken. My salvation and my honor depend on God; he is my mighty rock, my refuge. Trust in him at all times, you people; pour out your hearts to him, for God is our refuge."

Psalm 62:5-8 NIV

Let us each enter this New Year fully trusting in Our Lord to guide us. Let us each one declare that "He is my rock and my salvation; He is my fortress, I will not be shaken."

Have a blessed New Year!!

Bonnie

January 2

"My people, hear my teaching; listen to the words of my mouth. I will open my mouth with a parable; I will utter hidden things, things from of old -- things we have heard and known, things our ancestors have told us. We will not hide them from their descendants; we will tell the next generation the praiseworthy deeds of the Lord, his power, and the wonders he has done. He decreed statutes for Jacob and established the law in Israel, which he commanded our ancestors to teach their children, so the next generation would know them, even the children yet to be born, and they in turn would tell their children. Then they would put their trust in God and would not forget his deeds but would keep his commands. They would not be like their ancestors -- a stubborn and rebellious generation, whose hearts were not loyal to God, whose spirits were not faithful to him."

Psalms 78:1-8 NIV

Each time that a new year begins, we can view it as a renewed challenge (a resolution, if you will)...and there is not a much better resolution that to be "in The Word" DAILY!" Any reading plan is fine, as long as we are diligent.

Thank you for taking the time to read His Word along with me. Let's continue to "put our trust in God" and "tell the next generation."

Bonnie

January 3

"Remind the people to be subject to rulers and authorities, to be obedient, to be ready to do whatever is good, to slander no one, to be peaceable and considerate, and always to be gentle toward everyone. At one time we too were foolish, disobedient, deceived and enslaved by all kinds of passions and pleasures. We lived in malice and envy, being hated and hating one another. But when the kindness and love of God our Savior appeared, he saved us, not because of righteous things we had done, but because of his mercy."

Titus 3:1-5a NIV

Even in the midst of potential persecution and upheaval in government, the Apostle Paul offers these words of advice to his young protégé Titus. Surely these words of wisdom can apply to us today, as we seek to witness to others about the saving grace our God offers thru His Son Jesus. Nowhere in these verses does it say that it will always be easy, or that we will never be misunderstood! But these verses do outline how to be a good witness for our Lord! So let's "Remind the people...."

Bonnie

January 4

"Consider it pure joy, my brothers and sisters, whenever you face trials of many kinds, because you know that the testing of your faith produces perseverance. Let perseverance finish its work so that you may be mature and complete, not lacking anything. If any of you lacks wisdom, you should ask God, who gives generously to all without finding fault, and it will be given to you. But when you ask, you must believe and not doubt, because the one who doubts is like a wave of the sea, blown and tossed by the wind. That person should not expect to receive anything from the Lord. Such a person is double-minded and unstable in all they do."

James 1:2-8 NIV

If you know me well, you know that the book of James is my favorite Epistle. So full of Words of Wisdom! It's well worth your time to read the whole letter.

Bonnie

January 5

"My dear brothers and sisters, take note of this: Everyone should be quick to listen, slow to speak and slow to become angry, because human anger does not produce the righteousness that God desires. Therefore, get rid of all moral filth and the evil that is so prevalent and humbly accept the word planted in you, which can save you. Do not merely listen to the word, and so deceive yourselves. Do what it says."

James 1:19-22 NIV

This morning, after reading several good devotions, and a number of passages from both the Old and New Testament, I came right back here... for more words of wisdom that God shared with us through His servant James! Some very practical instructions are found right here in these verses. Praying that you and I would both would be "quick to listen, slow to speak, and slow to become angry!" ... THEN this crazy world will be a better place! So: "Do What It Says!"

Bonnie

January 6

"As long as the earth endures, seedtime and harvest, cold and heat, summer and winter, day and night will never cease."

Genesis 8:22 NIV

As I watched the snow gently falling this morning, I came across this simple poetic verse, and just wanted to share it with you····.. Take a moment today to share your thoughts with our great God. He is always listening.

Bonnie

January 7

"The righteous cry out, and the Lord hears them; he delivers them from all their troubles. The Lord is close to the brokenhearted and saves those who are crushed in spirit."

Psalms 34:17-18 NIV

Please note that these verses do not say that the righteousness will never have trouble or heartache. This says "The Lord is close to the broken-hearted." He listens to our cries for help. He is near. Our Lord knows our thoughts... our hurts... and our greatest joys! He Who endured the cross to save me, will walk with me, and talk with me, and carry me through it all.

Bonnie

January 8

Dearly beloved, avenge not yourselves, but rather give place unto wrath: for it is written, Vengeance is mine; I will repay, saith the Lord. Therefore if thine enemy hunger, feed him; if he thirst, give him drink: for in so doing thou shalt heap coals of fire on his head. Be not overcome of evil, but overcome evil with good."

Romans 12:17-21 KJV

The reason I am posting this in the old King James Version, is that I have precious memories of memorizing this passage that way in camp at Lake Springfield Christian Assembly many many years ago!! Generally though I prefer the NIV. Regardless... we all need to love one another and do our best to "overcome evil with good."

Bonnie

9.

Bonnie's Blessings

January 9

"Sing to the Lord, all the earth; proclaim his salvation day after day. Declare his glory among the nations, his marvelous deeds among all peoples. For great is the Lord and most worthy of praise; he is to be feared above all gods. For all the gods of the nations are idols, but the Lord made the heavens. Splendor and majesty are before him; strength and joy are in his dwelling place. Ascribe to the Lord, all you families of nations, ascribe to the Lord glory and strength. Ascribe to the Lord the glory due his name; bring an offering and come before him. Worship the Lord in the splendor of his holiness. Tremble before him, all the earth! The world is firmly established; it cannot be moved."

1 Chronicles 16:23-30 NIV

Wherever you may be, lift your heart and your voice...and Praise Him!!

Bonnie

10.

January 10

"Forget the former things; do not dwell on the past. See, I am doing a new thing! Now it springs up; do you not perceive it? I am making a way in the wilderness and streams in the wasteland."

Isaiah 43:18-19 NIV

It's so beautiful and reassuring, the way Our Lord cares for us! HE knows our thoughts and our heart's desires. We need to give this New Year to HIM, and let HIM direct our path and choices this year, and beyond.

Bonnie

January 11

"Be strong and very courageous. Be careful to obey all the law my servant Moses gave you; do not turn from it to the right or to the left, that you may be successful wherever you go. Keep this Book of the Law always on your lips; meditate on it day and night, so that you may be careful to do everything written in it. Then you will be prosperous and successful. Have I not commanded you? Be strong and courageous. Do not be afraid; do not be discouraged, for the Lord your God will be with you wherever you go."

Joshua 1:7-9 NIV

Whether you are crossing the street, or crossing the ocean to share the Message of God's Love.... this promise is sure... He Will Be With You!

Bonnie

January 12

"I will extol the Lord at all times; His praise will always be on my lips. I will glory in the Lord; let the afflicted hear and rejoice. Glorify the Lord with me; let us exalt His name together."

Psalms 34:1-3 NIV

◆·◆

Please read this whole Psalm, as I did this morning.... while listening to the song "Ever Be" by Bethel Music... And pray to The Almighty: "Faithful You have been; and Faithful You will be. You pledge Yourself to me. And that is why I sing: "Your praise will ever be on my lips!"

Bonnie

January 13

"Do you not know? Have you not heard? The Lord is the everlasting God, the Creator of the ends of the earth. He will not grow tired or weary, and his understanding no one can fathom. He gives strength to the weary and increases the power of the weak. Even youths grow tired and weary, and young men stumble and fall; but those who hope in the Lord will renew their strength. They will soar on wings like eagles; they will run and not grow weary, they will walk and not be faint."

Isaiah 40:28-31 NIV

So, let us not grow weary! Let up put our HOPE in The Lord!

14.

Bonnie

January 14

"You have searched me, Lord, and you know me. You know when I sit and when I rise; you perceive my thoughts from afar. You discern my going out and my lying down; you are familiar with all my ways. Before a word is on my tongue you, Lord, know it completely. You hem me in behind and before, and you lay your hand upon me. Such knowledge is too wonderful for me, too lofty for me to attain. Where can I go from your Spirit? Where can I flee from your presence? If I go up to the heavens, you are there; if I make my bed in the depths, you are there. If I rise on the wings of the dawn, if I settle on the far side of the sea, even there your hand will guide me, your right hand will hold me fast.

Psalms 139:1-10 NIV

As I have just finished a lovely weekend of celebrating my birthday with my dear family, and then a Sunday of worship, I also pondered my faltering memory issues, and appreciate the strong support I have from my family and therapist, and many friends..... Saying all this, to add that Our Great Compassionate God is THE ONE Who truly Knows me, and what a blessing to be reminded that HE CARES! His Hand guides us, and He "holds us fast!"

Happy
Birthday,
Bonnie!!

15.

Bonnie

January 15

"For this reason I kneel before the Father, from whom every family in heaven and on earth derives its name. I pray that out of his glorious riches he may strengthen you with power through his Spirit in your inner being, so that Christ may dwell in your hearts through faith. And I pray that you, being rooted and established in love, may have power, together with all the Lord's holy people, to grasp how wide and long and high and deep is the love of Christ, and to know this love that surpasses knowledge—that you may be filled to the measure of all the fullness of God."

Ephesians 3:14-19 NIV

I like to share this passage several times a year... such a beautiful prayer reminder... may Our Lord be very near to you today... and throughout this year!

Bonnie

January 16

"Let love and faithfulness never leave you; bind them around your neck, write them on the tablet of your heart. Then you will win favor and a good name in the sight of God and man. Trust in the Lord with all your heart and lean not on your own understanding; in all your ways submit to him, and he will make your paths straight. Do not be wise in your own eyes; fear the Lord and shun evil. This will bring health to your body and nourishment to your bones."

Proverbs 3:3-8 NIV

Even though I have always been surrounded by a loving family and very dear friends, I cannot imagine a good, contented life without The Lord as my Guide!

Bonnie

January 17

"Therefore each of you must put off falsehood and speak truthfully to your neighbor, for we are all members of one body. "In your anger do not sin": Do not let the sun go down while you are still angry, and do not give the devil a foothold. Anyone who has been stealing must steal no longer, but must work, doing something useful with their own hands, that they may have something to share with those in need. Do not let any unwholesome talk come out of your mouths, but only what is helpful for building others up according to their needs, that it may benefit those who listen. And do not grieve the Holy Spirit of God, with whom you were sealed for the day of redemption. Get rid of all bitterness, rage and anger, brawling and slander, along with every form of malice. Be kind and compassionate to one another, forgiving each other, just as in Christ God forgave you."

Ephesians 4:25-32 NIV

Praying you have a good, peaceful day!

Bonnie

18.

January 18

"But to you who are listening I say: Love your enemies, do good to those who hate you, bless those who curse you, pray for those who mistreat you. If someone slaps you on one cheek, turn to them the other also. If someone takes your coat, do not withhold your shirt from them. Give to everyone who asks you, and if anyone takes what belongs to you, do not demand it back. Do to others as you would have them do to you."

Luke 6:27-31 NIV

Wow!! I am sure that I do not consistently display an attitude this generous, to all people! I've got some work to do! How about you?

Bonnie

January 19

"Consider it pure joy, my brothers and sisters, whenever you face trials of many kinds, because you know that the testing of your faith produces perseverance. Let perseverance finish its work so that you may be mature and complete, not lacking anything. If any of you lacks wisdom, you should ask God, who gives generously to all without finding fault, and it will be given to you. But when you ask, you must believe and not doubt, because the one who doubts is like a wave of the sea, blown and tossed by the wind. That person should not expect to receive anything from the Lord. Such a person is double-minded and unstable in all they do."

James 1:2-8 NIV

If you know me well, you know that James is my favorite Epistle; it is filled with practical advice on how our Lord wants us to live.

Bonnie

January 20

"This is how we know that we live in him and he in us: He has given us of his Spirit. And we have seen and testify that the Father has sent his Son to be the Savior of the world. If anyone acknowledges that Jesus is the Son of God, God lives in them and they in God. And so we know and rely on the love God has for us. God is love. Whoever lives in love lives in God, and God in them. This is how love is made complete among us so that we will have confidence on the day of judgment: In this world we are like Jesus. There is no fear in love. But perfect love drives out fear, because fear has to do with punishment. The one who fears is not made perfect in love. We love because he first loved us. Whoever claims to love God yet hates a brother or sister is a liar. For whoever does not love their brother and sister, whom they have seen, cannot love God, whom they have not seen. And he has given us this command: Anyone who loves God must also love their brother and sister."

1 John 4:13-21 NIV

This whole chapter (actually, this whole Epistle) is a great way to start your day!

Bonnie

January 21

"Is anyone among you in trouble? Let them pray. Is anyone happy? Let them sing songs of praise. Is anyone among you sick? Let them call the elders of the church to pray over them and anoint them with oil in the name of the Lord. And the prayer offered in faith will make the sick person well; the Lord will raise them up. If they have sinned, they will be forgiven. Therefore confess your sins to each other and pray for each other so that you may be healed. The prayer of a righteous person is powerful and effective."

James 5:13-16 NIV

❖·❖

God is Good... All the Time!!

Bonnie

January 22

"Consider it pure joy, my brothers and sisters, whenever you face trials of many kinds, because you know that the testing of your faith produces perseverance. Let perseverance finish its work so that you may be mature and complete, not lacking anything. If any of you lacks wisdom, you should ask God, who gives generously to all without finding fault, and it will be given to you. But when you ask, you must believe and not doubt, because the one who doubts is like a wave of the sea, blown and tossed by the wind. That person should not expect to receive anything from the Lord. Such a person is double-minded and unstable in all they do. Believers in humble circumstances ought to take pride in their high position. But the rich should take pride in their humiliation—since they will pass away like a wild flower. For the sun rises with scorching heat and withers the plant; its blossom falls and its beauty is destroyed. In the same way, the rich will fade away even while they go about their business. Blessed is the one who perseveres under trial because, having stood the test, that person will receive the crown of life that the Lord has promised to those who love him."

James 1:2-12 NIV

❖·❖

More today from James, my favorite Epistle. Praying that we will each endure any difficulties that come our way, asking our Lord to fill us with wisdom!

Bonnie

23.

January 23

"Sing to the Lord a new song; sing to the Lord, all the earth. Sing to the Lord, praise his name; proclaim his salvation day after day. Declare his glory among the nations, his marvelous deeds among all peoples. For great is the Lord and most worthy of praise; he is to be feared above all gods. For all the gods of the nations are idols, but the Lord made the heavens. Splendor and majesty are before him; strength and glory are in his sanctuary. Ascribe to the Lord, all you families of nations, ascribe to the Lord glory and strength. Ascribe to the Lord the glory due his name; bring an offering and come into his courts. Worship the Lord in the splendor of his holiness; tremble before him, all the earth. Say among the nations, "The Lord reigns." The world is firmly established, it cannot be moved; he will judge the peoples with equity. Let the heavens rejoice, let the earth be glad; let the sea resound, and all that is in it. Let the fields be jubilant, and everything in them; let all the trees of the forest sing for joy. Let all creation rejoice before the Lord, for he comes, he comes to judge the earth. He will judge the world in righteousness and the peoples in his faithfulness."

Psalms 96:1-13 NIV

❖·❖

How amazing it is to worship the One True and Living God!

Bonnie

January 24

"Therefore, as God's chosen people, holy and dearly loved, clothe yourselves with compassion, kindness, humility, gentleness and patience. Bear with each other and forgive one another if any of you has a grievance against someone. Forgive as the Lord forgave you. And over all these virtues put on love, which binds them all together in perfect unity. Let the peace of Christ rule in your hearts, since as members of one body you were called to peace. And be thankful. Let the message of Christ dwell among you richly as you teach and admonish one another with all wisdom through psalms, hymns, and songs from the Spirit, singing to God with gratitude in your hearts. And whatever you do, whether in word or deed, do it all in the name of the Lord Jesus, giving thanks to God the Father through him."

Colossians 3:12-17 NIV

Praying you have a great week ahead of you, and whatever you plan to do..."Do it all in the name of the Lord Jesus, giving thanks to God through Him!"

Bonnie

25.

January 25

"As for me, I will always have hope; I will praise you more and more. My mouth will tell of your righteous deeds, of your saving acts all day long— though I know not how to relate them all. I will come and proclaim your mighty acts, Sovereign Lord; I will proclaim your righteous deeds, yours alone. Since my youth, God, you have taught me, and to this day I declare your marvelous deeds. Even when I am old and gray, do not forsake me, my God, till I declare your power to the next generation, your mighty acts to all who are to come."

Psalms 71:14-18 NIV

Oh, how I long for these verses to describe my life! Friends, our words and actions need to declare to the next generation that we worship a powerful God Who is full of Love!!

Bonnie

January 26

"Where then does wisdom come from? Where does understanding dwell? It is hidden from the eyes of every living thing, concealed even from the birds in the sky. Destruction and Death say, "Only a rumor of it has reached our ears." God understands the way to it and he alone knows where it dwells, for he views the ends of the earth and sees everything under the heavens. When he established the force of the wind and measured out the waters, when he made a decree for the rain and a path for the thunderstorm, then he looked at wisdom and appraised it; he confirmed it and tested it. And he said to the human race, "The fear of the Lord—that is wisdom, and to shun evil is understanding."

Job 28:20-28 NIV

Come, Friends! Let us fear the Lord and shun evil!!

Bonnie

January 27

"You have searched me, Lord, and you know me. You know when I sit and when I rise; you perceive my thoughts from afar. You discern my going out and my lying down; you are familiar with all my ways. Before a word is on my tongue you, Lord, know it completely. You hem me in behind and before, and you lay your hand upon me. Such knowledge is too wonderful for me, too lofty for me to attain. Where can I go from your Spirit? Where can I flee from your presence? If I go up to the heavens, you are there; if I make my bed in the depths, you are there. If I rise on the wings of the dawn, if I settle on the far side of the sea, even there your hand will guide me, your right hand will hold me fast.

Psalms 139:1-10 NIV

Someone else also needs this Psalm today as much as I did. Hope you are blessed by these Words…. that is my prayer.

Bonnie

January 28

"Finally, be strong in the Lord and in his mighty power. Put on the full armor of God, so that you can take your stand against the devil's schemes. For our struggle is not against flesh and blood, but against the rulers, against the authorities, against the powers of this dark world and against the spiritual forces of evil in the heavenly realms. Therefore put on the full armor of God, so that when the day of evil comes, you may be able to stand your ground, and after you have done everything, to stand. Stand firm then, with the belt of truth buckled around your waist, with the breastplate of righteousness in place, and with your feet fitted with the readiness that comes from the gospel of peace. In addition to all this, take up the shield of faith, with which you can extinguish all the flaming arrows of the evil one. Take the helmet of salvation and the sword of the Spirit, which is the word of God. And pray in the Spirit on all occasions with all kinds of prayers and requests."

Ephesians 6:10-18 NIV

Come, Friends! Let us fight!

One of the devotionals I read this morning centered on this familiar passage... I love to hear our AWANA students quoting it in unison! Indeed... WE all need to LIVE IT in unison!! Love the Lord and shun evil!!

Bonnie

January 29

"Because of the Lord's great love we are not consumed, for his compassions never fail. They are new every morning; great is your faithfulness."

Lamentations 3:22-23 NIV

These Words are TRUE....No Matter What!!

30.

Bonnie

January 30

"Why, my soul, are you downcast? Why so disturbed within me? Put your hope in God, for I will yet praise him, my Savior and my God."

Psalms 42:11 NIV

———— ◆·◆ ————

Anytime I feel really discouraged, this is one of my "go to" passages, and I encourage you to read the whole chapter.

Bonnie

31.

January 31

"For here we do not have an enduring city, but we are looking for the city that is to come. Through Jesus, therefore, let us continually offer to God a sacrifice of praise—the fruit of lips that openly profess his name. And do not forget to do good and to share with others, for with such sacrifices God is pleased. Have confidence in your leaders and submit to their authority, because they keep watch over you as those who must give an account. Do this so that their work will be a joy, not a burden, for that would be of no benefit to you."

Hebrews 13:14-17 NIV

I am looking forward to walking the Streets of Gold... but meanwhile (while we are still here on earth), let's "not forget to do good and share with others, for with such sacrifices God is pleased." These are encouraging Words, aren't they!?!

Bonnie

Bonnie and Bud with their grandchildren and great-grandchildren. When they first started taking pictures in front of the shark in the back they could all fit in the mouth of the shark.

"Children are a gift from the Lord; they are a reward from him."

Psalm 127:3

February

February 1

Hate what is evil; cling to what is good. Be devoted to one another in love. Honor one another above yourselves. Never be lacking in zeal, but keep your spiritual fervor, serving the Lord. Be joyful in hope, patient in affliction, faithful in prayer."

Romans 12:1-12 NIV

Good Morning! Today I read these Words out loud as I sat here with my coffee··· and I found it very encouraging··· especially the last sentence in verse 12. What great advice for how to live for The Lord!!

Bonnie

February 2

"I will exalt you, my God the King; I will praise your name for ever and ever. Every day I will praise you and extol your name for ever and ever. Great is the Lord and most worthy of praise; his greatness no one can fathom. One generation commends your works to another; they tell of your mighty acts. They speak of the glorious splendor of your majesty— and I will meditate on your wonderful works. They tell of the power of your awesome works— and I will proclaim your great deeds. They celebrate your abundant goodness and joyfully sing of your righteousness. The Lord is gracious and compassionate, slow to anger and rich in love. The Lord is good to all; he has compassion on all he has made. All your works praise you, Lord; your faithful people extol you. They tell of the glory of your kingdom and speak of your might, so that all people may know of your mighty acts and the glorious splendor of your kingdom.

Psalms 145:1-12 NIV

As I relished the marvelous poetry of this Psalm of Praise, I also gave pause at the comment "one generation commends your works to another. They tell of your mighty acts......and I will tell of Your great deeds..."..... And I asked myself "Am I truly focused on that amazing assignment to commend His works to others?!?" Please ask yourself this same question, and let's be Eagerly Diligent in carrying out this important task!!

Bonnie

February 3

"Cleanse me with hyssop, and I will be clean; wash me, and I will be whiter than snow. Let me hear joy and gladness; let the bones you have crushed rejoice. Hide your face from my sins and blot out all my iniquity. Create in me a pure heart, O God, and renew a steadfast spirit within me. Do not cast me from your presence or take your Holy Spirit from me. Restore to me the joy of your salvation and grant me a willing spirit, to sustain me."

Psalms 51:7-12 NIV

Praying everyone in the path of this winter weather can stay safe and warm. And grateful that our Lord has provided a way for our hearts and souls to the cleansed... "whiter than snow" thru the blood of Jesus!

Bonnie

February 4

"The Lord is good, a refuge in times of trouble. He cares for those who trust in him, but with an overwhelming flood he will make an end of Nineveh; he will pursue his foes into the realm of darkness."

Nahum 1:7-8 NIV

HE is a Good Good GOD! But He Does call us to TRUST and OBEY HIM!! And these verses do not declare that we won't have trouble! However, He is Our God, Who Cares! Lean on HIM!!   *Bonnie*

February 5

"Though the fig tree does not bud and there are no grapes on the vines, though the olive crop fails and the fields produce no food, though there are no sheep in the pen and no cattle in the stalls, yet I will rejoice in the Lord, I will be joyful in God my Savior. The Sovereign Lord is my strength; he makes my feet like the feet of a deer, he enables me to tread on the heights....

Habakkuk 3:17-19 NIV

Our great God is ultimately Lord of All··· No Matter What!! Let us be determined to Praise and Serve Him, and share the Good News that He has provided a Savior!

Bonnie

February 6

""God opposes the proud but shows favor to the humble." Humble yourselves, therefore, under God's mighty hand, that he may lift you up in due time. Cast all your anxiety on him because he cares for you."

1 Peter 5:5-7 NIV

"I know what it is to be in need, and I know what it is to have plenty. I have learned the secret of being content in any and every situation, whether well fed or hungry, whether living in plenty or in want. I can do all this through him who gives me strength."

Philippians 4:12-13 NIV

No Matter What your circumstances may be today.... The Lord Cares!! HE can provide the strength you need right now. Cast all your anxiety on Him, and He will Lift you up!!

Bonnie

February 7

"Come, let us sing for joy to the Lord; let us shout aloud to the Rock of our salvation. Let us come before him with thanksgiving and extol him with music and song. For the Lord is the great God, the great King above all gods. In his hand are the depths of the earth, and the mountain peaks belong to him. The sea is his, for he made it, and his hands formed the dry land. Come, let us bow down in worship, let us kneel before the Lord our Maker; for he is our God and we are the people of his pasture, the flock under his care.....

Psalms 95:1-7 NIV

Let's start our day praising Him for everything good He has done for us and for every blessing He has given us!!

Bonnie

February 8

"For I know the plans I have for you," declares the Lord,
"plans to prosper you and not to harm you, plans to give
you hope and a future. Then you will call on me and come
and pray to me, and I will listen to you. You will seek me
and find me when you seek me with all your heart."

Jeremiah 29:11-13 NIV

Let us continue daily to seek Him, and pray to Him... the One True
God...He promises to listen!

Bonnie

February 9

"The Lord is compassionate and gracious, slow to anger, abounding in love. He will not always accuse, nor will he harbor his anger forever; he does not treat us as our sins deserve or repay us according to our iniquities. For as high as the heavens are above the earth, so great is his love for those who fear him; as far as the east is from the west, so far has he removed our transgressions from us. As a father has compassion on his children, so the Lord has compassion on those who fear him; for he knows how we are formed, he remembers that we are dust. The life of mortals is like grass, they flourish like a flower of the field; the wind blows over it and it is gone, and its place remembers it no more. But from everlasting to everlasting the Lord's love is with those who fear him, and his righteousness with their children's children— with those who keep his covenant and remember to obey his precepts."

Psalms 103:8-18 NIV

These verses provide a beautiful reminder of how what an amazing, loving, compassionate God we serve! .... Yes, I am aware that not everyone has had a loving earthly father... but our God's Love is so great that He would even offer His own Son as the ultimate sacrifice so that you and I could be redeemed!! Let's praise Him and serve Him with gladness in our hearts today!!

Bonnie

February 10

"Hear what the Lord says to you, people of Israel. This is what the Lord says: "Do not learn the ways of the nations or be terrified by signs in the heavens, though the nations are terrified by them. For the practices of the peoples are worthless; they cut a tree out of the forest, and a craftsman shapes it with his chisel. They adorn it with silver and gold; they fasten it with hammer and nails so it will not totter. Like a scarecrow in a cucumber field, their idols cannot speak; they must be carried because they cannot walk. Do not fear them; they can do no harm nor can they do any good." No one is like you, Lord; you are great, and your name is mighty in power. Who should not fear you, King of the nations? This is your due. Among all the wise leaders of the nations and in all their kingdoms, there is no one like you."

Jeremiah 10:1-7 NIV

This whole chapter is amazing to read! We who have been taught the Truth of The Lord Almighty need to be anxious to share the Good News, near and far!!

Bonnie

February 11

"Do not fret because of those who are evil or be envious of those who do wrong; for like the grass they will soon wither, like green plants they will soon die away. Trust in the Lord and do good; dwell in the land and enjoy safe pasture. Take delight in the Lord, and he will give you the desires of your heart. Commit your way to the Lord; trust in him and he will do this: He will make your righteous reward shine like the dawn, your vindication like the noonday sun. Be still before the Lord and wait patiently for him; do not fret when people succeed in their ways, when they carry out their wicked schemes."

Psalms 37:1-7 NIV

Did you ever think "I try to do things right but I have all these problems... but those other people who don't even try to be nice, are living a rich happy life!"??? Read this whole chapter, because it addresses this exact situation! You are not the only one with such feelings, but truth is that GOD STILL CARES! HIS WAY is ultimately the right and good way. And HE is always ready to listen... you can even tell Him when you don't think that life is fair. The world wasn't very nice to Jesus either!! But ultimately HE AROSE! And He is still listening to our prayers today!!

Bonnie

"The end of all things is near. Therefore be alert and of sober mind so that you may pray. Above all, love each other deeply, because love covers over a multitude of sins. Offer hospitality to one another without grumbling. Each of you should use whatever gift you have received to serve others, as faithful stewards of God's grace in its various forms. If anyone speaks, they should do so as one who speaks the very words of God. If anyone serves, they should do so with the strength God provides, so that in all things God may be praised through Jesus Christ. To him be the glory and the power for ever and ever. Amen."

1 Peter 4:7-11 NIV

Every one of us can do these things to some extent! Read these verses again and consider what you can do, and what you are already doing to serve others, and to use whatever gifts the Lord has given you, "to serve others." Let your love for our God be evident in the life you live! Praise Him today with your words and with your actions. To God be the Glory! Amen.

Bonnie

45.

February 13

Have I not commanded you? Be strong and courageous. Do
not be afraid; do not be discouraged; for the Lord your God
will be with you wherever you go.

Joshua 1:9

You will keep in perfect peace those whose minds are
steadfast, because they trust You.

Isaiah 27:3

Let's Trust and Obey Him today!

Bonnie

February 14

"For God so loved the world that he gave his one and only Son, that whoever believes in him shall not perish but have eternal life. For God did not send his Son into the world to condemn the world, but to save the world through him. Whoever believes in him is not condemned, but whoever does not believe stands condemned already because they have not believed in the name of God's one and only Son. This is the verdict: Light has come into the world, but people loved darkness instead of light because their deeds were evil. Everyone who does evil hates the light, and will not come into the light for fear that their deeds will be exposed. But whoever lives by the truth comes into the light, so that it may be seen plainly that what they have done has been done in the sight of God."

John 3:16-21 NIV

—— ◆·◆ ——

Best True Love Story Ever

Bonnie

February 15

"May the God of hope fill you with all joy and peace as you trust in him, so that you may overflow with hope by the power of the Holy Spirit."

Romans 15:13 NIV

Praying that these Words from The Lord will provide Peace and Hope to each of us, No Matter What the circumstances may be at this moment in our lives!!

48.

Bonnie

February 16

"Finally, all of you, be like-minded, be sympathetic, love one another, be compassionate and humble. Do not repay evil with evil or insult with insult. On the contrary, repay evil with blessing, because to this you were called so that you may inherit a blessing. For, "Whoever would love life and see good days must keep their tongue from evil and their lips from deceitful speech. They must turn from evil and do good; they must seek peace and pursue it. For the eyes of the Lord are on the righteous and his ears are attentive to their prayer, but the face of the Lord is against those who do evil." Who is going to harm you if you are eager to do good? But even if you should suffer for what is right, you are blessed. "Do not fear their threats; do not be frightened." But in your hearts revere Christ as Lord. Always be prepared to give an answer to everyone who asks you to give the reason for the hope that you have. But do this with gentleness and respect, keeping a clear conscience, so that those who speak maliciously against your good behavior in Christ may be ashamed of their slander. For it is better, if it is God's will, to suffer for doing good than for doing evil."

1 Peter 3:8-17 NIV

These Words shared centuries ago with the believers, are still great Words of advice and encouragement to each of us today. This should be our attitude as we make our daily choices!

Bonnie

49.

February 17

"Anxiety weighs down the heart, but a kind word cheers it up."

Proverbs 12:25 NIV

"Do not be anxious about anything, but in every situation, by prayer and petition with thanksgiving, present your request to God. And the peace of God, which transcends all understanding, will guard your hearts and your minds in Christ Jesus."

Philippians 4:6-7 NIV

I especially like the phrase "in every situation"... because Our God Cares about everything in our lives... whether joys or sorrows!

Bonnie

February 18

"Let us hold unswervingly to the hope we profess, for he who promised is faithful. And let us consider how we may spur one another on toward love and good deeds, not giving up meeting together, as some are in the habit of doing, but encouraging one another—and all the more as you see the Day approaching."

Hebrews 10:23-25 NIV

"Carry each other's burdens, and in this way you will fulfill the law of Christ."

Galatians 6:2 NIV

Praying that this is how you and I would live out our lives··· Leaning on HIS Word, and willingly helping each other!

Bonnie

February 19

"He was despised and rejected by mankind, a man of suffering, and familiar with pain. Like one from whom people hide their faces he was despised, and we held him in low esteem. Surely he took up our pain and bore our suffering, yet we considered him punished by God, stricken by him, and afflicted. But he was pierced for our transgressions, he was crushed for our iniquities; the punishment that brought us peace was on him, and by his wounds we are healed. We all, like sheep, have gone astray, each of us has turned to our own way; and the Lord has laid on him the iniquity of us all."

Isaiah 53:3-6 NIV

Even though I cringe as I read these words... yet I also treasure these verses, because I have learned that Isaiah the Prophet was foretelling about Our Savior Jesus... Who was perfect and without sun... and yet He WILLINGLY offered HIMSELF as the Sacrifice to save ME ... and YOU.. from OUR SIN!!! He did NOT have to do that, you know!! He could have chosen to NOT go to the cruel cross!! But He chose to die in my place!! In Your Place!! So we could be forgiven of our sins, and have the opportunity to accept GRACE!! Hallelujah! I am free! We can sing that together because of Calvary!!

Bonnie

February 20

"Finally, be strong in the Lord and in his mighty power. Put on the full armor of God, so that you can take your stand against the devil's schemes. For our struggle is not against flesh and blood, but against the rulers, against the authorities, against the powers of this dark world and against the spiritual forces of evil in the heavenly realms. Therefore put on the full armor of God, so that when the day of evil comes, you may be able to stand your ground, and after you have done everything, to stand. Stand firm then, with the belt of truth buckled around your waist, with the breastplate of righteousness in place, and with your feet fitted with the readiness that comes from the gospel of peace. In addition to all this, take up the shield of faith, with which you can extinguish all the flaming arrows of the evil one. Take the helmet of salvation and the sword of the Spirit, which is the word of God. And pray in the Spirit on all occasions with all kinds of prayers and requests. With this in mind, be alert and always keep on praying for all the Lord's people."

Ephesians 6:10-18 NIV

We are literally in a battle against evil! And we can only win with God on our side!

Bonnie

February 21

"I lift up my eyes to the mountains— where does my help come from? My help comes from the Lord, the Maker of heaven and earth. He will not let your foot slip— he who watches over you will not slumber; indeed, he who watches over Israel will neither slumber nor sleep. The Lord watches over you— the Lord is your shade at your right hand; the sun will not harm you by day, nor the moon by night. The Lord will keep you from all harm— he will watch over your life; the Lord will watch over your coming and going both now and forevermore."

Psalms 121:1-8 NIV

Amen! Indeed! I simply cannot fathom life without The Lord! I pray that HE is also your comfort and guide and friend! My Lord and My Savior ··· now and forevermore!

Bonnie

54.

February 22

"Therefore encourage one another and build each other up, just as in fact you are doing. Now we ask you, brothers and sisters, to acknowledge those who work hard among you, who care for you in the Lord and who admonish you. Hold them in the highest regard in love because of their work. Live in peace with each other. And we urge you, brothers and sisters, warn those who are idle and disruptive, encourage the disheartened, help the weak, be patient with everyone. Make sure that nobody pays back wrong for wrong, but always strive to do what is good for each other and for everyone else. Rejoice always, pray continually, give thanks in all circumstances; for this is God's will for you in Christ Jesus."

1 Thessalonians 5:11-18 NIV

Such amazing Words of advice and encouragement that still are true today! So··· Be Encouraged··· And Be An Encourager!!

Bonnie

February 23

"For the word of God is alive and active. Sharper than any double-edged sword, it penetrates even to dividing soul and spirit, joints and marrow; it judges the thoughts and attitudes of the heart. Nothing in all creation is hidden from God's sight. Everything is uncovered and laid bare before the eyes of him to whom we must give account."

Hebrews 4:12-13 NIV

Therefore, let us be studying and obeying His Word; and following Jesus Christ, Who is "The Word Made Flesh"!

Bonnie

February 24

"Seek the Lord while he may be found; call on him while he is near. Let the wicked forsake their ways and the unrighteous their thoughts. Let them turn to the Lord, and he will have mercy on them, and to our God, for he will freely pardon. "For my thoughts are not your thoughts, neither are your ways my ways," declares the Lord. "As the heavens are higher than the earth, so are my ways higher than your ways and my thoughts than your thoughts. As the rain and the snow come down from heaven, and do not return to it without watering the earth and making it bud and flourish, so that it yields seed for the sower and bread for the eater, so is my word that goes out from my mouth: It will not return to me empty, but will accomplish what I desire and achieve the purpose for which I sent it. You will go out in joy and be led forth in peace; the mountains and hills will burst into song before you, and all the trees of the field will clap their hands. Instead of the thornbush will grow the juniper, and instead of briers the myrtle will grow. This will be for the Lord's renown, for an everlasting sign, that will endure forever."

Isaiah 55:6-13 NIV

As we journey out West with our kids and spouses, we are repeatedly reminded of the beauty of God's creation... and His unfailing Love for mankind. God is so good!

57.

Bonnie

February 25

"Do you not know? Have you not heard? The Lord is the everlasting God, the Creator of the ends of the earth. He will not grow tired or weary, and his understanding no one can fathom. He gives strength to the weary and increases the power of the weak. Even youths grow tired and weary, and young men stumble and fall; but those who hope in the Lord will renew their strength. They will soar on wings like eagles; they will run and not grow weary, they will walk and not be faint."

Isaiah 40:28-31 NIV

Once again amazed at the beauty of the views of God's great creation! However the weather conditions will prevent us from viewing most of the special sights of the Grand Canyon today. Enjoying our travels together.

Bonnie

February 25

"Praise be to the God and Father of our Lord Jesus Christ, who has blessed us in the heavenly realms with every spiritual blessing in Christ. For he chose us in him before the creation of the world to be holy and blameless in his sight. In love he predestined us for adoption to sonship through Jesus Christ, in accordance with his pleasure and will— to the praise of his glorious grace, which he has freely given us in the One he loves. In him we have redemption through his blood, the forgiveness of sins, in accordance with the riches of God's grace that he lavished on us. With all wisdom and understanding, he made known to us the mystery of his will according to his good pleasure, which he purposed in Christ, to be put into effect when the times reach their fulfillment—to bring unity to all things in heaven and on earth under Christ."

Ephesians 1:3-10 NIV

The same God Who created the majestic beautiful that we got a glimpse of our our vacation trip out West this week, is the God Who created you and me... He is the same God Who sent His only Son to this same earth to provide a way for us to be redeemed and one day spend Eternity with Him!! Thank You Lord!! We Praise You!!

Bonnie

February 26

"Do you not know? Have you not heard? The Lord is the everlasting God, the Creator of the ends of the earth. He will not grow tired or weary, and his understanding no one can fathom. He gives strength to the weary and increases the power of the weak. Even youths grow tired and weary, and young men stumble and fall; but those who hope in the Lord will renew their strength. They will soar on wings like eagles; they will run and not grow weary, they will walk and not be faint."

Isaiah 40:28-31 NIV

Once again amazed at the beauty of the views of God's great creation! However the weather conditions will prevent us from viewing most of the special sights of the Grand Canyon today. Enjoying our travels together.   *Bonnie*

February 27

"Therefore, as God's chosen people, holy and dearly loved, clothe yourselves with compassion, kindness, humility, gentleness and patience. Bear with each other and forgive one another if any of you has a grievance against someone. Forgive as the Lord forgave you. And over all these virtues put on love, which binds them all together in perfect unity. Let the peace of Christ rule in your hearts, since as members of one body you were called to peace. And be thankful. Let the message of Christ dwell among you richly as you teach and admonish one another with all wisdom through psalms, hymns, and songs from the Spirit, singing to God with gratitude in your hearts. And whatever you do, whether in word or deed, do it all in the name of the Lord Jesus, giving thanks to God the Father through him."

Colossians 3:12-17 NIV

What a beautiful description of how we should live each day! Praying that Peace of Christ truly dwells in your heart and that you may be full of Thanks today!

Bonnie

February 28

"Look, I am coming soon! My reward is with me, and I will give to each person according to what they have done. I am the Alpha and the Omega, the First and the Last, the Beginning and the End. "Blessed are those who wash their robes, that they may have the right to the tree of life and may go through the gates into the city. Outside are the dogs, those who practice magic arts, the sexually immoral, the murderers, the idolaters and everyone who loves and practices falsehood. "I, Jesus, have sent my angel to give you this testimony for the churches. I am the Root and the Offspring of David, and the bright Morning Star." The Spirit and the bride say, "Come!" And let the one who hears say, "Come!" Let the one who is thirsty come; and let the one who wishes take the free gift of the water of life."

Revelation 22:12-17 NIV

As we look forward to His return, we need to consistently alert others to do the same!!

Bonnie

Bonnie's Blessings

This photo was taken at the ocean in Korea...when we were a missionary family there. I LOVED collecting shells on a day like this.

Mother Maxine Seggelke made most of our clothes...otherwise they were often from some of the shipments of used clothing sent over from supporting churches!! I mostly like to wear genuine Korean outfits to church and other outings...I still have a few of them!

Bonnie

March

March 1

"Children's children are a crown to the aged, and parents are the pride of their children."

Proverbs 17:6 NIV

———— ◆•◆ ————

Bud and I are on our way with our own children, to a hospital in Arkansas to await the arrival of our newest great-grandchild!

Bonnie

March 2

"For I am not ashamed of the gospel, because it is the power of God that brings salvation to everyone who believes: first to the Jew, then to the Gentile. For in the gospel the righteousness of God is revealed—a righteousness that is by faith from first to last, just as it is written: "The righteous will live by faith." The wrath of God is being revealed from heaven against all the godlessness and wickedness of people, who suppress the truth by their wickedness, since what may be known about God is plain to them, because God has made it plain to them. For since the creation of the world God's invisible qualities—his eternal power and divine nature—have been clearly seen, being understood from what has been made, so that people are without excuse."

Romans 1:16-20 NIV

Lord, help us to boldly share the Good News to all who will listen!

Bonnie

March 3

"My dear brothers and sisters, take note of this: Everyone should be quick to listen, slow to speak and slow to become angry, because human anger does not produce the righteousness that God desires. Therefore, get rid of all moral filth and the evil that is so prevalent and humbly accept the word planted in you, which can save you. Do not merely listen to the word, and so deceive yourselves. Do what it says. Anyone who listens to the word but does not do what it says is like someone who looks at his face in a mirror and, after looking at himself, goes away and immediately forgets what he looks like. But whoever looks intently into the perfect law that gives freedom, and continues in it—not forgetting what they have heard, but doing it—they will be blessed in what they do. Those who consider themselves religious and yet do not keep a tight rein on their tongues deceive themselves, and their religion is worthless. Religion that God our Father accepts as pure and faultless is this: to look after orphans and widows in their distress and to keep oneself from being polluted by the world."

James 1:19-27 NIV

— ❖·❖ —

James is my "go to" Epistle. So many words of advice and encouragement. Praying these verses will encourage you today.

Bonnie

March 4

"He reached down from on high and took hold of me; he drew me out of deep waters. He rescued me from my powerful enemy, from my foes, who were too strong for me. They confronted me in the day of my disaster, but the Lord was my support. He brought me out into a spacious place; he rescued me because he delighted in me. The Lord has dealt with me according to my righteousness; according to the cleanness of my hands he has rewarded me. For I have kept the ways of the Lord; I am not guilty of turning from my God. All his laws are before me; I have not turned away from his decrees. I have been blameless before him and have kept myself from sin. The Lord has rewarded me according to my righteousness, according to the cleanness of my hands in his sight. To the faithful you show yourself faithful, to the blameless you show yourself blameless, to the pure you show yourself pure, but to the devious you show yourself shrewd. You save the humble but bring low those whose eyes are haughty. You, Lord, keep my lamp burning; my God turns my darkness into light.

Psalms 18:16-36 NIV

What a Mighty God we serve!

Bonnie

March 5

"Blessed is the one who perseveres under trial because, having stood the test, that person will receive the crown of life that the Lord has promised to those who love him."

James 1:12 NIV

"Not only so, but we also glory in our sufferings, because we know that suffering produces perseverance; perseverance, character; and character, hope. And hope does not put us to shame, because God's love has been poured out into our hearts through the Holy Spirit, who has been given to us."

Romans 5:3-5 NIV

———◆•◆———

These two passages seem to speak to the state of things happening in our world today!!

Bonnie

March 6

"Consider it pure joy, my brothers and sisters, whenever you face trials of many kinds, because you know that the testing of your faith produces perseverance. Let perseverance finish its work so that you may be mature and complete, not lacking anything. If any of you lacks wisdom, you should ask God, who gives generously to all without finding fault, and it will be given to you. But when you ask, you must believe and not doubt, because the one who doubts is like a wave of the sea, blown and tossed by the wind. That person should not expect to receive anything from the Lord. Such a person is double-minded and unstable in all they do."

James 1:2-8 NIV

Good morning! I am starting it off with one of my favorite passages... this letter from James is so practical and encouraging... well worth reading the whole epistle in one sitting. Let us "persevere" no matter what our circumstances! 70. *Bonnie*

March 7

"There is a time for everything, and a season for every activity under the heavens: a time to be born and a time to die, a time to plant and a time to uproot, a time to kill and a time to heal, a time to tear down and a time to build, a time to weep and a time to laugh, a time to mourn and a time to dance, a time to scatter stones and a time to gather them, a time to embrace and a time to refrain from embracing, a time to search and a time to give up, a time to keep and a time to throw away, a time to tear and a time to mend, a time to be silent and a time to speak, a time to love and a time to hate, a time for war and a time for peace. What do workers gain from their toil? I have seen the burden God has laid on the human race. He has made everything beautiful in its time. He has also set eternity in the human heart; yet no one can fathom what God has done from beginning to end. I know that there is nothing better for people than to be happy and to do good while they live."

Ecclesiastes 3:1-12 NIV

Lifting Praises to Our God for His Goodness!

Bonnie

March 8

"Do not be deceived: God cannot be mocked. A man reaps what he sows. Whoever sows to please their flesh, from the flesh will reap destruction; whoever sows to please the Spirit, from the Spirit will reap eternal life. Let us not become weary in doing good, for at the proper time we will reap a harvest if we do not give up. Therefore, as we have opportunity, let us do good to all people, especially to those who belong to the family of believers."

Galatians 6:7-10 NIV

Sharing a special passage that a dear friend sent to me yesterday.... and reminding you that I always welcome anyone to send me a favorite Scripture or devotional thought. May The Lord bless you this day!

Bonnie

March 9

"May the God of hope fill you with all joy and peace as you trust in him, so that you may overflow with hope by the power of the Holy Spirit."

Romans 15:13 NIV

"For I know the plans I have for you," declares the Lord, "plans to prosper you and not to harm you, plans to give you hope and a future. Then you will call on me and come and pray to me, and I will listen to you. You will seek me and find me when you seek me with all your heart."

Jeremiah 29:11-13 NIV

Surely I am not the only one who keeps hoping for a better tomorrow! For improvement in my own life, but also for the many around me who seem to be struggling. And also for this world full of so many who openly declare they do not even believe in The Lord God and His Son Jesus!

Bonnie

March 10

"All praise to God, the Father of our Lord Jesus Christ. God is our merciful Father and the source of all comfort. He comforts us in all our troubles so that we can comfort others. When they are troubled, we will be able to give them the same comfort God has given us. For the more we suffer for Christ, the more God will shower us with his comfort through Christ. Even when we are weighed down with troubles, it is for your comfort and salvation! For when we ourselves are comforted, we will certainly comfort you. Then you can patiently endure the same things we suffer. We are confident that as you share in our sufferings, you will also share in the comfort God gives us."

2 Corinthians 1:3-7 NLT

There is so much that we can learn from those who have gone before us. Let's each make an effort to encourage others with God's precious promises.

Bonnie

March 11

"Finally, be strong in the Lord and in his mighty power. Put on the full armor of God, so that you can take your stand against the devil's schemes. For our struggle is not against flesh and blood, but against the rulers, against the authorities, against the powers of this dark world and against the spiritual forces of evil in the heavenly realms. Therefore put on the full armor of God, so that when the day of evil comes, you may be able to stand your ground, and after you have done everything, to stand. Stand firm then, with the belt of truth buckled around your waist, with the breastplate of righteousness in place, and with your feet fitted with the readiness that comes from the gospel of peace. In addition to all this, take up the shield of faith, with which you can extinguish all the flaming arrows of the evil one. Take the helmet of salvation and the sword of the Spirit, which is the word of God."

Ephesians 6:10-17 NIV

Simply put, there is no way that I can manage to face all of "the forces of evil" in this world on my own! The Lord is my shield and my Guide! His Word is Truth, and I simply MUST depend upon the Wisdom found there! It is my prayer today that YOU can "Be Strong In The Lord" !!

Bonnie

March 12

"Peace I leave with you; my peace I give you. I do not give to you as the world gives. Do not let your hearts be troubled and do not be afraid."

John 14:27 NIV

These words that Jesus spoke to His disciples before He ascended still ring true today. A devotional that I read said: "Failure is a stepping stone on the journey to success. It is not to be feared, but to be learned from. Fear is only a set back if you allow it to be so. God is greater than your fear of failure."---David Villa

Bonnie

March 13

[The Lord declared to Joshua]: "No one will be able to stand against you all the days of your life. As I was with Moses, so I will be with you; I will never leave you nor forsake you. Be strong and courageous, because you will lead these people to inherit the land I swore to their ancestors to give them. "Be strong and very courageous. Be careful to obey all the law my servant Moses gave you; do not turn from it to the right or to the left, that you may be successful wherever you go."

Joshua 1:5-7 NIV

[The Apostle Paul advised the early Christians] "Be on your guard; stand firm in the faith; be courageous; be strong. Do everything in love."

1 Corinthians 16:13-14 NIV

This same God Who spoke these Words to Joshua and Paul, is ready and willing to lead you and me through the battles of life as well!

Bonnie

March 14

"No, in all these things we are more than conquerors through him who loved us. For I am convinced that neither death nor life, neither angels nor demons, neither the present nor the future, nor any powers, neither height nor depth, nor anything else in all creation, will be able to separate us from the love of God that is in Christ Jesus our Lord."

Romans 8:37-39 NIV

It is well worth the time to read all of this chapter, as we dedicate this day to worship and praise of our Creator...Lord...Savior!! Let's Gladly Worship and Serve Him Today!!

Bonnie

March 15

Then Jesus came to them and said, "All authority in heaven and on earth has been given to me. Therefore go and make disciples of all nations, baptizing them in the name of the Father and of the Son and of the Holy Spirit, and teaching them to obey everything I have commanded you. And surely I am with you always, to the very end of the age.""

Matthew 28:18-20 NIV

My parents not only helped me to memorize these verses at a very young age, but also were obedient to this call to action. I clearly remember them lining up my three brothers and me in the kitchen for an important Family Meeting... They referred to these verses, and talked about people in a far away country who needed to hear the Good News about Jesus. They felt compelled to answer the call to share that Gospel with the people in Korea who were in the midst of recovering from a terrible war. But there was still a more universal war to be won—— the battle against SIN. Some of them had not yet heard about Jesus. And on that day, we agreed as a family to go to the mission field. Several years later, it was obvious that some of the most diligent co-workers in that effort, were our fellow Korean brothers and sisters in Christ! There are so many ways to respond to "The Great Commission" in these verses. Listen to whatever The Lord is laying on your heart today.

Bonnie

79.

March 15

"Let us, then, go to him outside the camp, bearing the disgrace he bore. For here we do not have an enduring city, but we are looking for the city that is to come. Through Jesus, therefore, let us continually offer to God a sacrifice of praise—the fruit of lips that openly profess his name. And do not forget to do good and to share with others, for with such sacrifices God is pleased. Have confidence in your leaders and submit to their authority, because they keep watch over you as those who must give an account. Do this so that their work will be a joy, not a burden, for that would be of no benefit to you. Pray for us. We are sure that we have a clear conscience and desire to live honorably in every way. I particularly urge you to pray so that I may be restored to you soon. Now may the God of peace, who through the blood of the eternal covenant brought back from the dead our Lord Jesus, that great Shepherd of the sheep, equip you with everything good for doing his will, and may he work in us what is pleasing to him, through Jesus Christ, to whom be glory for ever and ever. Amen."

Hebrews 13:13-21 NIV

Don't stop there··· read more in this great chapter. ··· Equip Yourself!! Do HIS WILL in your life; live to please The Lord, and Give Glory to HIM!

Bonnie

March 16

"Blessed is the one who does not walk in step with the wicked or stand in the way that sinners take or sit in the company of mockers, but whose delight is in the law of the Lord, and who meditates on his law day and night. That person is like a tree planted by streams of water, which yields its fruit in season and whose leaf does not wither— whatever they do prospers. Not so the wicked! They are like chaff that the wind blows away. Therefore the wicked will not stand in the judgment, nor sinners in the assembly of the righteous. For the Lord watches over the way of the righteous, but the way of the wicked leads to destruction."

Psalms 1:1-6 NIV

[How reassuring and comforting to know that The Lord Himself is "watching over me"! This gives me such peace in the midst of any problems or turmoil in my life. And I pray that you find that same reassurance in His Word today.

Bonnie

March 17

"All our days pass away under your wrath; we finish our years with a moan. Our days may come to seventy years, or eighty, if our strength endures; yet the best of them are but trouble and sorrow, for they quickly pass, and we fly away. If only we knew the power of your anger! Your wrath is as great as the fear that is your due. Teach us to number our days, that we may gain a heart of wisdom. Relent, Lord! How long will it be? Have compassion on your servants. Satisfy us in the morning with your unfailing love, that we may sing for joy and be glad all our days. Make us glad for as many days as you have afflicted us, for as many years as we have seen trouble. May your deeds be shown to your servants, your splendor to their children. May the favor of the Lord our God rest on us; establish the work of our hands for us— yes, establish the work of our hands."

Psalms 90:9-17 NIV

My simple prayer today is that we would each seek "the favor of our Lord God" and be eager to serve Him with "the work of our hands."

Bonnie

March 18

"What causes fights and quarrels among you? Don't they come from your desires that battle within you? You desire but do not have, so you kill. You covet but you cannot get what you want, so you quarrel and fight. You do not have because you do not ask God. When you ask, you do not receive, because you ask with wrong motives, that you may spend what you get on your pleasures. You adulterous people, don't you know that friendship with the world means enmity against God? Therefore, anyone who chooses to be a friend of the world becomes an enemy of God. Or do you think Scripture says without reason that he jealously longs for the spirit he has caused to dwell in us? But he gives us more grace. That is why Scripture says: "God opposes the proud but shows favor to the humble." Submit yourselves, then, to God. Resist the devil, and he will flee from you. Come near to God and he will come near to you. Wash your hands, you sinners, and purify your hearts, you double-minded. Grieve, mourn and wail. Change your laughter to mourning and your joy to gloom. Humble yourselves before the Lord, and he will lift you up."
James 4:1-10 NIV

—— ◆·◆ ——

If I have been sharing with you for very long, you know how much I treasure James' Epistle, which is packed full of wisdom and practical advice... as in these verses today. Let us "humble ourselves", dear ones!!

Bonnie

83.

March 19

"Three times I pleaded with the Lord to take it away from me. But he said to me, "My grace is sufficient for you, for my power is made perfect in weakness." Therefore I will boast all the more gladly about my weaknesses, so that Christ's power may rest on me. That is why, for Christ's sake, I delight in weaknesses, in insults, in hardships, in persecutions, in difficulties. For when I am weak, then I am strong."

2 Corinthians 12:8-10 NIV

The great Apostle Paul wrote these words concerning his extreme problems··· What a great example for each of us to follow. Remember: HIS GRACE IS SUFFICIENT!

Bonnie

March 20

"Therefore if you have any encouragement from being united with Christ, if any comfort from his love, if any common sharing in the Spirit, if any tenderness and compassion, then make my joy complete by being like-minded, having the same love, being one in spirit and of one mind. Do nothing out of selfish ambition or vain conceit. Rather, in humility value others above yourselves, not looking to your own interests but each of you to the interests of the others. In your relationships with one another, have the same mindset as Christ Jesus: Who, being in very nature God, did not consider equality with God something to be used to his own advantage; rather, he made himself nothing by taking the very nature of a servant, being made in human likeness. And being found in appearance as a man, he humbled himself by becoming obedient to death— even death on a cross!"

Philippians 2:1-8 NIV

Hoping you have a blessed day.

Bonnie

March 21

"I am reminded of your sincere faith, which first lived in your grandmother Lois and in your mother Eunice and, I am persuaded, now lives in you also. For this reason I remind you to fan into flame the gift of God, which is in you through the laying on of my hands. For the Spirit God gave us does not make us timid, but gives us power, love and self-discipline. So do not be ashamed of the testimony about our Lord or of me his prisoner. Rather, join with me in suffering for the gospel, by the power of God. He has saved us and called us to a holy life—not because of anything we have done but because of his own purpose and grace. This grace was given us in Christ Jesus before the beginning of time, but it has now been revealed through the appearing of our Savior, Christ Jesus, who has destroyed death and has brought life and immortality to light through the gospel. And of this gospel I was appointed a herald and an apostle and a teacher. That is why I am suffering as I am. Yet this is no cause for shame, because I know whom I have believed, and am convinced that he is able to guard what I have entrusted to him until that day."

2 Timothy 1:5-12 NIV.

These beautiful verses are part of a Letter written by the Apostle Paul from prison, to a young man who had studied under him.   86.   Bonnie

March 22

"For though we live in the world, we do not wage war as the world does. The weapons we fight with are not the weapons of the world. On the contrary, they have divine power to demolish strongholds. We demolish arguments and every pretension that sets itself up against the knowledge of God, and we take captive every thought to make it obedient to Christ."

2 Corinthians 10:3-5 NIV

Our Lord is The Answer and Solution for every problem in this world! Let us follow this directive to make every thought obedient to Christ!! When we do that, we will NOT be dwelling on anger or hatred or greed or lust!! We will instead be dwelling on how to help others, and how to Praise the Lord with our thoughts, words, and actions!

Bonnie

March 23

"For though we live in the world, we do not wage war as the world does. The weapons we fight with are not the weapons of the world. On the contrary, they have divine power to demolish strongholds. We demolish arguments and every pretension that sets itself up against the knowledge of God, and we take captive every thought to make it obedient to Christ."

2 Corinthians 10:3-5 NIV

Our Lord is The Answer and Solution for every problem in this world! Let us follow this directive to make every thought obedient to Christ!! When we do that, we will NOT be dwelling on anger or hatred or greed or lust!! We will instead be dwelling on how to help others, and how to Praise the Lord with our thoughts, words, and actions! *Bonnie*

March 24

"People swear by someone greater than themselves, and the oath confirms what is said and puts an end to all argument. Because God wanted to make the unchanging nature of his purpose very clear to the heirs of what was promised, he confirmed it with an oath. God did this so that, by two unchangeable things in which it is impossible for God to lie, we who have fled to take hold of the hope set before us may be greatly encouraged. We have this hope as an anchor for the soul, firm and secure. It enters the inner sanctuary behind the curtain, where our forerunner, Jesus, has entered on our behalf. He has become a high priest forever, in the order of Melchizedek."

Hebrews 6:16-20 NIV

As the great Hymn remind us..." Will your anchor hold in the storms of life? When the clouds unfold their wings of strife? When the strong tides lift and the cables strain, will your anchor drift or firm remain? ··· We have an Anchor that keeps the soul steadfast and sure while the billows roll! Fastened to The Rock which cannot move; Grounded firm and deep in The Savior's Love!" ... Let us "hold fast" to that anchor this week!!

Bonnie

March 25

"Do not love the world or anything in the world. If anyone loves the world, love for the Father is not in them. For everything in the world—the lust of the flesh, the lust of the eyes, and the pride of life—comes not from the Father but from the world. The world and its desires pass away, but whoever does the will of God lives forever."

1 John 2:15-17 NIV

Remember, dear friends··· GOD IS LOVE!

Bonnie

March 26

"For I know the plans I have for you," declares the Lord, "plans to prosper you and not to harm you, plans to give you hope and a future. Then you will call on me and come and pray to me, and I will listen to you. You will seek me and find me when you seek me with all your heart."

Jeremiah 29:11-13 NIV

Never tire of reading or sharing these beautiful Words of encouragement!

Bonnie

March 27

"Shout for joy to God, all the earth! Sing the glory of his name; make his praise glorious. Say to God, "How awesome are your deeds! So great is your power that your enemies cringe before you. All the earth bows down to you; they sing praise to you, they sing the praises of your name." Come and see what God has done, his awesome deeds for mankind! He turned the sea into dry land, they passed through the waters on foot— come, let us rejoice in him. He rules forever by his power, his eyes watch the nations— let not the rebellious rise up against him. Praise our God, all peoples, let the sound of his praise be heard;"

Psalms 66:1-8 NIV

Let us be united in Praise to The One True God, as did the Israelites of old. HE Who gave His Son to save us, knows you, and calls you by name!!!

Bonnie

March 28

"You will keep in perfect peace those whose minds are steadfast, because they trust in you. Trust in the Lord forever, for the Lord, the Lord himself, is the Rock eternal."

Isaiah 26:3-4 NIV

No Matter What caused the turmoil... HE can bring you Perfect Peace!

Bonnie

March 29

"Sing to the Lord a new song, for he has done marvelous things; his right hand and his holy arm have worked salvation for him. The Lord has made his salvation known and revealed his righteousness to the nations. He has remembered his love and his faithfulness to Israel; all the ends of the earth have seen the salvation of our God. Shout for joy to the Lord, all the earth, burst into jubilant song with music; make music to the Lord with the harp, with the harp and the sound of singing, with trumpets and the blast of the ram's horn— shout for joy before the Lord, the King. Let the sea resound, and everything in it, the world, and all who live in it. Let the rivers clap their hands, let the mountains sing together for joy; let them sing before the Lord, for he comes to judge the earth. He will judge the world in righteousness and the peoples with equity."

Psalms 98:1-9 NIV

This is a beautiful Psalm to read aloud, as a prayer of praise to the Lord! (That's what I just did, before sending this to you). Have a great day! Our God is so good!

Bonnie

94.

March 30

"Give praise to the Lord, proclaim his name; make known among the nations what he has done. Sing to him, sing praise to him; tell of all his wonderful acts. Glory in his holy name; let the hearts of those who seek the Lord rejoice. Look to the Lord and his strength; seek his face always."

1 Chronicles 16:8-11 NIV

[Especially grateful today for those who give of themselves to help spread this Good News "among the nations" of what God has done to provide the way for salvation.

Bonnie

March 31

"Now the Lord is the Spirit, and where the Spirit of the Lord is, there is freedom. And we all, who with unveiled faces contemplate the Lord's glory, are being transformed into his image with ever-increasing glory, which comes from the Lord, who is the Spirit."

2 Corinthians 3:17-18 NIV

This is my desire... to be fully "transformed into His image!" This whole chapter... this whole letter to the Corinthians... is amazing!] ... Have a great Sunday worshiping Our Lord

Bonnie

JUL   62

I clearly remember this day on Grandpa Mike's farm...and the matching dresses that Mother had ordered for us (usually she made our outfits). This was the summer after we returned from South Korea.

April

April 1

"Jesus answered, "I am the way and the truth and the life. No one comes to the Father except through me. If you really know me, you will know my Father as well. From now on, you do know him and have seen him.""

John 14:6-7 NIV

◆·◆

What an amazing statement! ... One which must be shared!... With The Whole World!

Bonnie

April 2

"Therefore, since we are surrounded by such a great cloud of witnesses, let us throw off everything that hinders and the sin that so easily entangles. And let us run with perseverance the race marked out for us, fixing our eyes on Jesus, the pioneer and perfecter of faith. For the joy set before him he endured the cross, scorning its shame, and sat down at the right hand of the throne of God. Consider him who endured such opposition from sinners, so that you will not grow weary and lose heart."

Hebrews 12:1-3 NIV

Praying that these verses will encourage you today, no matter what your circumstance may be, and that you "will not grow weary and lose heart!"

Bonnie

100.

April 3

"So he left them and went away once more and prayed the third time, saying the same thing. Then he returned to the disciples and said to them, "Are you still sleeping and resting? Look, the hour has come, and the Son of Man is delivered into the hands of sinners. Rise! Let us go! Here comes my betrayer!""

Matthew 26:44-46 NIV

Sadly, I am certain that I would have been one of Jesus' followers who fell asleep while Jesus was praying so intensely! May Our Lord give us hearts that are earnestly alert to His calling!

Bonnie

April 4

"Save us, Lord our God, and gather us from the nations, that we may give thanks to your holy name and glory in your praise. Praise be to the Lord, the God of Israel, from everlasting to everlasting. Let all the people say, "Amen!" Praise the Lord."

Psalms 106:47-48 NIV

◆·◆

Oh, that all peoples would recognize and praise The One True Living God, and Praise Him!!

Bonnie

April 5

"My dear brothers and sisters, take note of this: Everyone should be quick to listen, slow to speak and slow to become angry, because human anger does not produce the righteousness that God desires. Therefore, get rid of all moral filth and the evil that is so prevalent and humbly accept the word planted in you, which can save you. Do not merely listen to the word, and so deceive yourselves. Do what it says. Anyone who listens to the word but does not do what it says is like someone who looks at his face in a mirror and, after looking at himself, goes away and immediately forgets what he looks like. But whoever looks intently into the perfect law that gives freedom, and continues in it—not forgetting what they have heard, but doing it—they will be blessed in what they do."

James 1:19-25 NIV

Words of Wisdom from my favorite Epistle. "Do What It Says!"

Bonnie

April 6

"Remind the people to be subject to rulers and authorities, to be obedient, to be ready to do whatever is good, to slander no one, to be peaceable and considerate, and always to be gentle toward everyone."

Titus 3:1-2 NIV

Greetings! I had agreed some time ago to be an election judge again, so I needed to arrive at the Polling Place by 5:30a.m., and my responsibilities do not end until Well AFTER the polls close (at 5:30), and then we deliver all the ballots and other documentation and equipment to the courthouse in Mt Vernon.] I say this to preface my disappointment in how few citizens have taken advantage of the freedom and opportunity offered to them today. Meanwhile in many parts of the world, such freedoms are totally crushed!! (And I acknowledge there are many things that legitimately keep individuals from being able to follow thru.) Anyway let's FOCUS on rejoicing in the amazing freedom that we have in Christ!! Amen

Bonnie

104.

Bonnie's Blessings

April 7

"My people, hear my teaching; listen to the words of my mouth. I will open my mouth with a parable; I will utter hidden things, things from of old— things we have heard and known, things our ancestors have told us. We will not hide them from their descendants; we will tell the next generation the praiseworthy deeds of the Lord, his power, and the wonders he has done. He decreed statutes for Jacob and established the law in Israel, which he commanded our ancestors to teach their children, so the next generation would know them, even the children yet to be born, and they in turn would tell their children. Then they would put their trust in God and would not forget his deeds but would keep his commands."

Psalms 78:1-7 NIV

✦•✦

God's Word provides wisdom and guidance; peace and joy for the heart; truth and trust; redemption and salvation; confidence and courage; edification and the responsibility to pass it on to the next generation! Thank You, Lord!!

Bonnie

The hymn "Be Still My Soul, The Lord is on Thy Side" was just playing on a music link and that is my prayer for all of you.

April 8

"Keep your servant from willful sins; may they not rule over me. Then I will be blameless, innocent of transgression."

Psalm 19:13 NIV

One devotional writer commented: "To sin deliberately or arrogantly is dangerous. A sinful habit leads to addiction. People believe they can stop sinning whenever they want but many have been snared and fallen. .... With God's help, we find grace to break free and begin on the journey of recovery." The writer refers also to the old Hymn by Horatio R Palmer: Yield Not To Temptation. (You can look that up online or in an old Hymnal.) ... I pray that each of us will take these words to heart.

Bonnie

April 9

"Now may the Lord of peace himself give you peace at all times and in every way. The Lord be with all of you."

2 Thessalonians 3:16 NIV

—————— ✦·✦ ——————

Let us "soak in" His Peace today, and let Our God guide us through all our trials and triumphs!!

Bonnie

EXTRA THOUGHTS...

One of the devotions I read this morning closed by suggesting praying The Lord's Prayer aloud. ... I did that by reading it aloud from The King James Version, with fond memories of learning it as a child, from the Bible my parents had given me for my 8th birthday. This started a flood of beautiful reminders of my childhood. I am well aware that many people in my life did NOT grow up in such a secure loving environment... far from it!! HOWEVER, each adult can make a choice, daily, to provide an atmosphere of love and kindness to the people in their own home and surroundings. Our God Is Able to provide the strength to attain such a goal]...... "After this manner therefore pray ye: Our Father which art in heaven, Hallowed be thy name. Thy kingdom come. Thy will be done in earth, as it is in heaven. Give us this day our daily bread. And forgive us our debts, as we forgive our debtors. And lead us not into temptation, but deliver us from evil: For thine is the kingdom, and the power, and the glory, for ever. Amen."

Matthew 6:9–13 KJV

April 10

"Though the fig tree does not bud and there are no grapes on the vines, though the olive crop fails and the fields produce no food, though there are no sheep in the pen and no cattle in the stalls, yet I will rejoice in the Lord, I will be joyful in God my Savior. The Sovereign Lord is my strength; He makes my feet like the feet of a deer, he enables me to tread on the heights."

Habakkuk 3:17-18 NIV

When difficult times arise, as they will in everyone's life story, we must remember thaT Our God is still on His Throne. And He still hears and answers our prayers. Do not blame Him for your heartaches... but you can still cry out to Him about your troubles! And trust Him to provide an answer... even if it was not the answer you expected or hoped for. I know this in my own life. HIS WAYS are always better than my little plans or my big dreams!! THANK YOU, My Lord and King, for always listening and always caring!

Bonnie

April 11

"So do not worry, saying, 'What shall we eat?' or 'What shall we drink?' or 'What shall we wear?' For the pagans run after all these things, and your heavenly Father knows that you need them. But seek first his kingdom and his righteousness, and all these things will be given to you as well. Therefore do not worry about tomorrow, for tomorrow will worry about itself. Each day has enough trouble of its own."

Matthew 6:31-34 NIV

❖·❖

This morning I slept a bit later than usual, and then I got busy with various things around the house I needed to do; they were all good things, but not urgent, and NOT anything to take priority over being in God's Word. So distracted that in my mind, I assumed that I had already done my Bible reading, and texting verses. Then one sweet friend messaged me that she missed getting Bible verses this morning from me, and she hoped I was okay. Wow!! I checked my phone, and saw that I had NOT sent ANY this morning!! So, the Lord had provided a gentle reminder about priorities!! So let's all first seek His Kingdom, and all the other things will get done eventually! (Bonnie's Version!) Sending Love n Prayers...

Bonnie

April 12

"He was despised and rejected by mankind, a man of suffering, and familiar with pain. Like one from whom people hide their faces he was despised, and we held him in low esteem. Surely he took up our pain and bore our suffering, yet we considered him punished by God, stricken by him, and afflicted. But he was pierced for our transgressions, he was crushed for our iniquities; the punishment that brought us peace was on him, and by his wounds we are healed. We all, like sheep, have gone astray, each of us has turned to our own way; and the Lord has laid on him the iniquity of us all."

Isaiah 53:3-6 NIV

◆•◆

Our Lord's sacrifice was prophesied long before the event. Christ knew what suffering was awaiting Him, but He did it anyway!! We can never repay Him! But we can love Him... obey Him...serve Him!!

Bonnie

April 13

"Therefore, since we are surrounded by such a great cloud of witnesses, let us throw off everything that hinders and the sin that so easily entangles. And let us run with perseverance the race marked out for us, fixing our eyes on Jesus, the pioneer and perfecter of faith. For the joy set before him he endured the cross, scorning its shame, and sat down at the right hand of the throne of God. Consider him who endured such opposition from sinners, so that you will not grow weary and lose heart."

Hebrews 12:1-3 NIV

Today Bud and I plan to attend sports events in Indiana, to watch two of our grandsons as they push themselves to do their best and win in their sports. Likewise we each have a challenge set before us , in our lives... to endure whatever hardships we are facing in order to display to others the importance of completing the task God has set in our hearts to do for Him, testifying that He is Lord and Savior. Let's "fix our eyes on Jesus" and not grow weary or lose heart! Do not be discouraged! It will be worth it all when we see Jesus! *Bonnie*

April 14

"While they were eating, Jesus took bread, and when he had given thanks, he broke it and gave it to his disciples, saying, "Take and eat; this is my body." Then he took a cup, and when he had given thanks, he gave it to them, saying, "Drink from it, all of you. This is my blood of the covenant, which is poured out for many for the forgiveness of sins. I tell you, I will not drink from this fruit of the vine from now on until that day when I drink it new with you in my Father's kingdom." When they had sung a hymn, they went out to the Mount of Olives

Matthew 26:26-30 NIV

Last nite at GCC, it was a very special reenactment that our Youth Group portrayed of this crucial nite in Christ's life here on earth. A great reminder that His Love for us took Him to the cross! He did not have to suffer and die in my place...but rather He "poured out His Blood" .... to wash away my sins!! THANK YOU, LORD!!

Bonnie

April 15

"They went to a place called Gethsemane, and Jesus said to his disciples, "Sit here while I pray." He took Peter, James and John along with him, and he began to be deeply distressed and troubled. "My soul is overwhelmed with sorrow to the point of death," he said to them. "Stay here and keep watch."

Mark 14:32-34 NIV.

I cannot read this dramatic passage without recalling the amazing group trip that Bud and I were able to take to The Holy Land. To stand there in The Garden, and listen to this Scripture read aloud, tore at my heart!! To think that Our Lord prayed these words, and surrendered Himself... for you and for me!!!!... is beyond comprehension!! Surely all we can do now is to thank Him, praise Him, and share the news of Him, and what He has done for us!!!

Bonnie

114.

April 16

""Do not store up for yourselves treasures on earth, where moths and vermin destroy, and where thieves break in and steal. But store up for yourselves treasures in heaven, where moths and vermin do not destroy, and where thieves do not break in and steal. For where your treasure is, there your heart will be also. "The eye is the lamp of the body. If your eyes are healthy, your whole body will be full of light. But if your eyes are unhealthy, your whole body will be full of darkness. If then the light within you is darkness, how great is that darkness! "No one can serve two masters. Either you will hate the one and love the other, or you will be devoted to the one and despise the other. You cannot serve both God and money."

Matthew 6:19-24 NIV

His Word is quite clear about this matter··· We need to keep our priorities in order! Let us seek to Put God First. Love and Serve Him!

Bonnie

April 17

"After the Sabbath, at dawn on the first day of the week, Mary Magdalene and the other Mary went to look at the tomb. There was a violent earthquake, for an angel of the Lord came down from heaven and, going to the tomb, rolled back the stone and sat on it. His appearance was like lightning, and his clothes were white as snow. The guards were so afraid of him that they shook and became like dead men. The angel said to the women, "Do not be afraid, for I know that you are looking for Jesus, who was crucified. He is not here; he has risen, just as he said. Come and see the place where he lay. Then go quickly and tell his disciples: 'He has risen from the dead and is going ahead of you into Galilee. There you will see him.' Now I have told you." So the women hurried away from the tomb, afraid yet filled with joy, and ran to tell his disciples. Suddenly Jesus met them. "Greetings," he said. They came to him, clasped his feet and worshiped him. Then Jesus said to them, "Do not be afraid. Go and tell my brothers to go to Galilee; there they will see me.""

Matthew 28:1-10 NIV

✦·✦

"HALLELUJAH!!! HE is RISEN indeed!!"

Bonnie

April 18

"You, Lord, showed favor to your land; you restored the fortunes of Jacob. You forgave the iniquity of your people and covered all their sins. You set aside all your wrath and turned from your fierce anger. Restore us again, God our Savior, and put away your displeasure toward us. Will you be angry with us forever? Will you prolong your anger through all generations? Will you not revive us again, that your people may rejoice in you? Show us your unfailing love, Lord, and grant us your salvation. I will listen to what God the Lord says; he promises peace to his people, his faithful servants— but let them not turn to folly. Surely his salvation is near those who fear him, that his glory may dwell in our land. Love and faithfulness meet together; righteousness and peace kiss each other. Faithfulness springs forth from the earth, and righteousness looks down from heaven. The Lord will indeed give what is good, and our land will yield its harvest. Righteousness goes before him and prepares the way for his steps."

Psalms 85:1-13 NIV.

This reminds me of lyrics from an old hymn: "Revive us again; Fill each heart with Thy love. May each soul be rekindled with fire from above!"

Bonnie

April 19

"Do you not know that in a race all the runners run, but only one gets the prize? Run in such a way as to get the prize. Everyone who competes in the games goes into strict training. They do it to get a crown that will not last, but we do it to get a crown that will last forever. Therefore I do not run like someone running aimlessly; I do not fight like a boxer beating the air. No, I strike a blow to my body and make it my slave so that after I have preached to others, I myself will not be disqualified for the prize."

1 Corinthians 9:24-27 NIV

❖◦❖

While I myself have never been a good athlete, I do hope to strive to run the race of life with determination... keeping my eyes set on the prize of eternal life with our Lord and Savior! Thank You, Jesus!!

Bonnie

April 20

"The Lord is my shepherd, I lack nothing. He makes me lie down in green pastures, he leads me beside quiet waters, he refreshes my soul. He guides me along the right paths for his name's sake. Even though I walk through the darkest valley, I will fear no evil, for you are with me; your rod and your staff, they comfort me. You prepare a table before me in the presence of my enemies. You anoint my head with oil; my cup overflows. Surely your goodness and love will follow me all the days of my life, and I will dwell in the house of the Lord forever."

Psalms 23:1-6 NIV

What Precious Words to start off our day! Come, let us follow The Good Shepherd together!

Sheep crossing our path...I loved this!

Bonnie

119.

Picture taken by Bonnie while visiting the Holy Land.

April 21

"Give praise to the Lord, proclaim his name; make known among the nations what he has done. Sing to him, sing praise to him; tell of all his wonderful acts. Glory in his holy name; let the hearts of those who seek the Lord rejoice. Look to the Lord and his strength; seek his face always.

Psalms 105:1-4 NIV

What Precious Words to start off our day! Come, let us follow The Good Shepherd together!

From my very earliest childhood memories, worshipping the Lord in His House on Sunday had top priority; and if bad weather or poor health prevented us from gathering at the church building, we still took time to worship.. even if we watched a service on TV or had a special family devotion time while my brothers and I took turns reading from the Bible and sang "Jesus Loves Me" together with our devoted parents. Now as adults, this responsibility is on our shoulders, so that His Truths will be passed on "for a thousand generations!"

Bonnie

120.

April 22

"Then Jesus came to them and said, "All authority in heaven and on earth has been given to me. Therefore go and make disciples of all nations, baptizing them in the name of the Father and of the Son and of the Holy Spirit, and teaching them to obey everything I have commanded you. And surely I am with you always, to the very end of the age.""

Matthew 28:18-20 NIV

———— ◆·◆ ————

These are the words of Jesus following His resurrection, as He was about to return to heaven; and His Commission applies to you and me as well: "Go and make disciples of all nations..." We've got a Big Job to do, friends! A Major Assignment! A Great Commission! Let's get busy... for Jesus!!

Bonnie

"For the word of God is alive and active. Sharper than any double-edged sword, it penetrates even to dividing soul and spirit, joints and marrow; it judges the thoughts and attitudes of the heart. Nothing in all creation is hidden from God's sight. Everything is uncovered and laid bare before the eyes of him to whom we must give account. Therefore, since we have a great high priest who has ascended into heaven, Jesus the Son of God, let us hold firmly to the faith we profess. For we do not have a high priest who is unable to empathize with our weaknesses, but we have one who has been tempted in every way, just as we are—yet he did not sin. Let us then approach God's throne of grace with confidence, so that we may receive mercy and find grace to help us in our time of need."

Hebrews 4:12-16 NIV

How amazing that our great God Who created us, also invites us to approach His Throne with our praises, and our requests!

Bonnie

April 24

"Love must be sincere. Hate what is evil; cling to what is good. Be devoted to one another in love. Honor one another above yourselves. Never be lacking in zeal, but keep your spiritual fervor, serving the Lord. Be joyful in hope, patient in affliction, faithful in prayer. Share with the Lord's people who are in need. Practice hospitality. Bless those who persecute you; bless and do not curse. Rejoice with those who rejoice; mourn with those who mourn. Live in harmony with one another. Do not be proud, but be willing to associate with people of low position. Do not be conceited. Do not repay anyone evil for evil. Be careful to do what is right in the eyes of everyone. If it is possible, as far as it depends on you, live at peace with everyone."

Romans 12:9-18 NIV

Such a beautiful description of how we as Christians should behave and live our lives!! Definitely worth reading the whole chapter!

Bonnie

April 25

"Do not be deceived: God cannot be mocked. A man reaps what he sows. Whoever sows to please their flesh, from the flesh will reap destruction; whoever sows to please the Spirit, from the Spirit will reap eternal life. Let us not become weary in doing good, for at the proper time we will reap a harvest if we do not give up. Therefore, as we have opportunity, let us do good to all people, especially to those who belong to the family of believers."

Galatians 6:7-10 NIV

As a farmer's wife, I am keenly aware of the term "reap what you sow." And I need to ask myself regularly if my efforts and my focus are centered of goals for a bountiful harvest for The Kingdom!??! Or do I spend most of my time, efforts, and money on meaningless projects? Each one of us will need to give our answers to God Himself.

Corn Harvest 2018 has begun on Klockenga Farms and the best part is father and son doing it together! Praising God for His Blessings!!

Bonnie

April 26

Consider these thoughts together: "Those who know Your Name trust in You, for You, Lord, have never forsaken those who seek You"... "When I am afraid, I put my trust in You."..."I seek You with all my heart; do not let me stray from Your commands."..."And we know that in all things God works for the good of those who love Him, who have been called according to His purpose"..."Blessed is the one who perseveres under trial because, having stood the test, that person will receive the crown of life that the Lord has promised those who love Him."

.[Psalm 9:10, Psalm 56:3, Psalm 119:10, Romans 8:28, James1:12 NIV]

Isn't this beautiful and encouraging!?! I did not organize these verses together myself... I copied this idea from a devotional. God's Word brings so much Light and Truth into our lives!! Praise Him!!

Bonnie

"Consider it pure joy, my brothers and sisters, whenever you face trials of many kinds, because you know that the testing of your faith produces perseverance. Let perseverance finish its work so that you may be mature and complete, not lacking anything. If any of you lacks wisdom, you should ask God, who gives generously to all without finding fault, and it will be given to you. But when you ask, you must believe and not doubt, because the one who doubts is like a wave of the sea, blown and tossed by the wind. That person should not expect to receive anything from the Lord. Such a person is double-minded and unstable in all they do. Believers in humble circumstances ought to take pride in their high position. But the rich should take pride in their humiliation—since they will pass away like a wild flower. For the sun rises with scorching heat and withers the plant; its blossom falls and its beauty is destroyed. In the same way, the rich will fade away even while they go about their business.

James 1:2-11 NIV

When we get to heaven, one of the many things I hope to do is take a long walk with James and listen to him sharing these words of wisdom... it is well worth your time to pause and read his whole letter in one sitting.. then contemplate on it the rest of the day or evening!

Bonnie

126.

April 28

"I will make them and the places surrounding my hill a blessing. I will send down showers in season; there will be showers of blessing. The trees will yield their fruit and the ground will yield its crops; the people will be secure in their land. They will know that I am the Lord, when I break the bars of their yoke and rescue them from the hands of those who enslaved them. They will no longer be plundered by the nations, nor will wild animals devour them. They will live in safety, and no one will make them afraid. I will provide for them a land renowned for its crops, and they will no longer be victims of famine in the land or bear the scorn of the nations. Then they will know that I, the Lord their God, am with them and that they, the Israelites, are my people, declares the Sovereign Lord. You are my sheep, the sheep of my pasture, and I am your God, declares the Sovereign Lord.'"

Ezekiel 34:26-31 NIV

———— ◆·◆ ————

In these verses, The Lord is obviously speaking to the Israelites thru His prophet Ezekiel... however we today can also lift up prayers for revival in our own hearts and lives... asking Him for Showers of Blessings! As I did that myself this morning, I also Googled the old hymn "Showers of Blessings" and sang along with the choir! You may choose to do that too!

Bonnie

127.

April 29

"I remember the days of long ago; I meditate on all your works and consider what your hands have done. I spread out my hands to you; I thirst for you like a parched land. Answer me quickly, Lord; my spirit fails. Do not hide your face from me or I will be like those who go down to the pit. Let the morning bring me word of your unfailing love, for I have put my trust in you. Show me the way I should go, for to you I entrust my life. Rescue me from my enemies, Lord, for I hide myself in you. Teach me to do your will, for you are my God; may your good Spirit lead me on level ground. For your name's sake, Lord, preserve my life; in your righteousness, bring me out of trouble."

Psalms 143:5-11 NIV

———— ◆•◆ ————

Whether you are weary or rejoicing today, it is encouraging to read the Psalms!

128.

Bonnie

April 30

"Shout for joy to the Lord, all the earth. Worship the Lord with gladness; come before him with joyful songs. Know that the Lord is God. It is he who made us, and we are his; we are his people, the sheep of his pasture. Enter his gates with thanksgiving and his courts with praise; give thanks to him and praise his name. For the Lord is good and his love endures forever; his faithfulness continues through all generations."

Psalms 100:1-5 NIV

This week Bud and I have done a lot of reminiscing... it happens every spring, as we think of our mothers, and their birthdays... and that leads to memories of what amazing parents we were both blessed with, who would strive so hard to seek God's Will in all their choices. Bud and I were each the oldest in our families and have been able to see through their examples that "the Lord is good and his love endures forever..."

This precious lady is my mother

It was not until sometime after I married Bud that I realized my mother-in-law was truly a "Proverbs 31 Woman" ! In every part of her life, Hope Klockenga thought of others first, and shared the Love of God! Plus, not having daughters of her own, she treated Janis and me like princesses! Such a blessing to have known her as "Mom" .

Bonnie

129.

May

May 1

"David praised the Lord in the presence of the whole assembly, saying, "Praise be to you, Lord, the God of our father Israel, from everlasting to everlasting. Yours, Lord, is the greatness and the power and the glory and the majesty and the splendor, for everything in heaven and earth is yours. Yours, Lord, is the kingdom; you are exalted as head over all. Wealth and honor come from you; you are the ruler of all things. In your hands are strength and power to exalt and give strength to all. Now, our God, we give you thanks, and praise your glorious name."

1 Chronicles 29:10-13 NIV

Lord, May all we say and do bring honor and praise to You, the One True God! May even our very lives be an offering to You!

"Happy Birthday in Heaven"

131.

Bonnie

May 2

"But since we belong to the day, let us be sober, putting on faith and love as a breastplate, and the hope of salvation as a helmet. For God did not appoint us to suffer wrath but to receive salvation through our Lord Jesus Christ. He died for us so that, whether we are awake or asleep, we may live together with him. Therefore encourage one another and build each other up, just as in fact you are doing."

1 Thessalonians 5:8-11 NIV

I would suggest you find time to read this whole chapter... or indeed the whole epistle! Meanwhile... I pray that you each have a good day... and Encourage Someone Today!

Bonnie

May 3

"What, then, shall we say in response to these things? If God is for us, who can be against us? He who did not spare his own Son, but gave him up for us all—how will he not also, along with him, graciously give us all things? Who will bring any charge against those whom God has chosen? It is God who justifies. Who then is the one who condemns? No one. Christ Jesus who died—more than that, who was raised to life—is at the right hand of God and is also interceding for us. Who shall separate us from the love of Christ? Shall trouble or hardship or persecution or famine or nakedness or danger or sword? As it is written: "For your sake we face death all day long; we are considered as sheep to be slaughtered." No, in all these things we are more than conquerors through him who loved us. For I am convinced that neither death nor life, neither angels nor demons, neither the present nor the future, nor any powers, neither height nor depth, nor anything else in all creation, will be able to separate us from the love of God that is in Christ Jesus our Lord."

Romans 8:31-39 NIV

In the midst of all the tragic news reports of the horrific things that some people are inflicting on their fellow mankind, my mind keeps returning to these verses in Romans... written when terrible things were also being done, even in broad daylight!!

Bonnie

133.

May 4

"This is what the Lord says— your Redeemer, the Holy One of Israel: "For your sake I will send to Babylon and bring down as fugitives all the Babylonians, in the ships in which they took pride. I am the Lord, your Holy One, Israel's Creator, your King." This is what the Lord says— he who made a way through the sea, a path through the mighty waters, who drew out the chariots and horses, the army and reinforcements together, and they lay there, never to rise again, extinguished, snuffed out like a wick: "Forget the former things; do not dwell on the past. See, I am doing a new thing! Now it springs up; do you not perceive it? I am making a way in the wilderness and streams in the wasteland. The wild animals honor me, the jackals and the owls, because I provide water in the wilderness and streams in the wasteland, to give drink to my people, my chosen, the people I formed for myself that they may proclaim my praise."

Isaiah 43:14-21 NIV

The Prophet Isaiah is here reminding the Israelites of times when The Lord rescued them from their captors; yet this is also a reminder that He sent Jesus to rescue us from our sinful life ... to redeem and refresh us! There is a better way! We do not need to dwell on the problems of the past... The Lord offers us fresh Living Water...Streams in the Wastelands... "Streams in the Desert!!"   134.

Bonnie

May 5

"The Lord is good, a refuge in times of trouble. He cares for those who trust in him..."

Nahum 1:7 NIV

Did you notice that this doesn't say we won't have trouble?!? However He cares for us when we trust Him...Keep the Faith, friends, thru happy times and "times of trouble." God is Our Refuge!

Bonnie

May 6

"Rejoice in the Lord always. I will say it again: Rejoice! Let your gentleness be evident to all. The Lord is near. Do not be anxious about anything, but in every situation, by prayer and petition, with thanksgiving, present your requests to God. And the peace of God, which transcends all understanding, will guard your hearts and your minds in Christ Jesus. Finally, brothers and sisters, whatever is true, whatever is noble, whatever is right, whatever is pure, whatever is lovely, whatever is admirable—if anything is excellent or praiseworthy—think about such things."

Philippians 4:4-8 NIV

Dear ones, I have shared this several times over the last few months, but these Words just really reach into my very soul, and perhaps it speaks to you also. "Let us rejoice!" And "not be anxious about anything!" We Serve a Great God, Who Cares!!

Bonnie

May 7

"May the God of hope fill you with all joy and peace as you trust in him, so that you may overflow with hope by the power of the Holy Spirit."

Romans 15:13 NIV

———— ◆•◆ ————

This evening we will be at a funeral visitation for one of Bud's younger cousins... it feels strange when you have to bid farewell to one who is younger... like we did with Bud's only brother Don several years ago... just "doesn't seem right"... but God in His Wisdom and with His Strength and Blessings, guides us through such times.] Meanwhile we are lifting up others who are bidding Farewell to loved ones way too young to be placed in the grave!! May our "God of Hope" ease the pain in those hearts especially!   137.   *Bonnie*

May 8

"I will exalt you, my God the King; I will praise your name for ever and ever. Every day I will praise you and extol your name for ever and ever. Great is the Lord and most worthy of praise; his greatness no one can fathom. One generation commends your works to another; they tell of your mighty acts. They speak of the glorious splendor of your majesty— and I will meditate on your wonderful works. They tell of the power of your awesome works— and I will proclaim your great deeds. They celebrate your abundant goodness and joyfully sing of your righteousness. The Lord is gracious and compassionate, slow to anger and rich in love. The Lord is good to all; he has compassion on all he has made. All your works praise you, Lord; your faithful people extol you. They tell of the glory of your kingdom and speak of your might, so that all people may know of your mighty acts and the glorious splendor of your kingdom. Your kingdom is an everlasting kingdom, and your dominion endures through all generations."

Psalms 145:1-13 NIV

This is a favorite for me, among many of the Psalms... but especially verses 3–5, as we approach Mother's Day, and I smile at the heritage that Bud and I enjoy from our parents... and strive to pass on to others! Our God is so good....

ALWAYS!   138.   *Bonnie*

May 9

"Love is patient, love is kind. It does not envy, it does not boast, it is not proud. It does not dishonor others, it is not self-seeking, it is not easily angered, it keeps no record of wrongs. Love does not delight in evil but rejoices with the truth. It always protects, always trusts, always hopes, always perseveres."

1 Corinthians 13:4-7 NIV

These precious familiar verses are appropriate when describing a Christian mother... and I was blessed with one of the very best; so was my Bud. Whatever your situation may be, I hope that this will be a Happy Mother's Day! Praying the Lord will continue to bless you, as you lean on Him and focus on His Word.

Bonnie

139.

May 10

"Let the peace of Christ rule in your hearts, since as members of one body you were called to peace. And be thankful. Let the message of Christ dwell among you richly as you teach and admonish one another with all wisdom through psalms, hymns, and songs from the Spirit, singing to God with gratitude in your hearts. And whatever you do, whether in word or deed, do it all in the name of the Lord Jesus, giving thanks to God the Father through him

Colossians 3:15-17 NIV

As we celebrate the graduates (of all ages) in our various families, I pray that "whatever you do in word or deed", each will seek to be a witness of God's love and salvation. There is no greater goal at any age or stage in life. And today we are thankful!

Bonnie

140.

May 11

"My son, do not forget my teaching, but keep my commands in your heart, for they will prolong your life many years and bring you peace and prosperity. Let love and faithfulness never leave you; bind them around your neck, write them on the tablet of your heart. Then you will win favor and a good name in the sight of God and man. Trust in the Lord with all your heart and lean not on your own understanding; in all your ways submit to him, and he will make your paths straight."

Proverbs 3:1-6 NIV

One of the devotionals I was reading this morning led me to Proverbs 3 (a favorite); the Lord shares so much wisdom through the Words in Proverbs. [A number of friends that I have looked up to over the years have a practice of reading a chapter in Proverbs each day... which works out neatly, since there are 31 chapters in that book!] ... God's Words are True... so "write them on the tablet of your heart!!"

Bonnie

May 12

"Why do you complain, Jacob? Why do you say, Israel, "My way is hidden from the Lord; my cause is disregarded by my God"? Do you not know? Have you not heard? The Lord is the everlasting God, the Creator of the ends of the earth. He will not grow tired or weary, and his understanding no one can fathom. He gives strength to the weary and increases the power of the weak. Even youths grow tired and weary, and young men stumble and fall; but those who hope in the Lord will renew their strength. They will soar on wings like eagles; they will run and not grow weary, they will walk and not be faint."

Isaiah 40:27-31 NIV

Let us lean on HIM for our strength and guidance through this day! He is The Everlasting God!!

142.

Bonnie

May 13

"For the Word of God is alive and active. Sharper than any double-edged sword, it penetrates even to dividing soul and spirit, joints and marrow; it judges the thoughts and attitudes of the heart. Nothing in all creation is hidden from God's sight. Everything is uncovered and laid bare before the eyes of him to whom we must give account. Therefore, since we have a great high priest who has ascended into heaven, Jesus the Son of God, let us hold firmly to the faith we profess. For we do not have a high priest who is unable to empathize with our weaknesses, but we have one who has been tempted in every way, just as we are—yet he did not sin. Let us then approach God's throne of grace with confidence, so that we may receive mercy and find grace to help us in our time of need."

Hebrews 4:12-16 NIV

My own weaknesses are many!! Yet I serve a loving God Who is all-knowing...and He Still Loves me... and when I open my heart and soul to my Maker, and turn to Him for help and healing... He responds with His tender Mercy and Grace!! That's how I can still have Peace in the midst of Turmoil. And the Good News is that HIS ARMS are open wide to receive anyone who will submit to His Plan. Thank You, Lord!!

Bonnie

May 14

"In the same way, you who are younger, submit yourselves to your elders. All of you, clothe yourselves with humility toward one another, because, "God opposes the proud but shows favor to the humble." Humble yourselves, therefore, under God's mighty hand, that he may lift you up in due time. Cast all your anxiety on him because he cares for you. Be alert and of sober mind. Your enemy the devil prowls around like a roaring lion looking for someone to devour. Resist him, standing firm in the faith, because you know that the family of believers throughout the world is undergoing the same kind of sufferings. And the God of all grace, who called you to his eternal glory in Christ, after you have suffered a little while, will himself restore you and make you strong, firm and steadfast. To him be the power for ever and ever. Amen."

1 Peter 5:5-11 NIV

Although these words were penned years ago, they still apply to us today. Our God Who created us knows our hearts and minds, and He is ready and willing to help us, no matter what is troubling our minds, hearts, or physical bodies. He Cares!

Bonnie

144.

May 15

"The Lord is my shepherd, I lack nothing. He makes me lie down in green pastures, he leads me beside quiet waters, he refreshes my soul. He guides me along the right paths for his name's sake. Even though I walk through the darkest valley, I will fear no evil, for you are with me; your rod and your staff, they comfort me. You prepare a table before me in the presence of my enemies. You anoint my head with oil; my cup overflows. Surely your goodness and love will follow me all the days of my life, and I will dwell in the house of the Lord forever."

Psalms 23:1-6 NIV

This special passage is meaningful on any given day. In our family today we are doing more celebrating of our graduates, especially Hannah today at John and Dianna's house; then we will soon also be celebrating our other graduates in Indiana! It is good to acknowledge that Our Lord is good... all the time... no matter what!! Praise Him all the days of your life!

Bonnie

145.

May 16

As for you, see that what you have heard from the beginning remains in you. If it does, you also will remain in the Son and in the Father. And this is what he promised us —eternal life."

1 John 2:24-25 NIV

This special passage is meaningful on any given day. In our family today we are doing more celebrating of our graduates, especially Hannah today at John and Dianna's house; then we will soon also be celebrating our other graduates in Indiana! It is good to acknowledge that Our Lord is good... all the time... no matter what!! Praise Him all the days of your life!

Bonnie

May 17

"Therefore we do not lose heart. Though outwardly we are wasting away, yet inwardly we are being renewed day by day. For our light and momentary troubles are achieving for us an eternal glory that far outweighs them all. So we fix our eyes not on what is seen, but on what is unseen, since what is seen is temporary, but what is unseen is eternal

2 Corinthians 4:16-18 NIV

Actually of course the whole chapter is worth reading!] Have a great day, keeping your eyes fixed on Jesus!

Bonnie

May 18

"Now we ask you, brothers and sisters, to acknowledge those who work hard among you, who care for you in the Lord and who admonish you. Hold them in the highest regard in love because of their work. Live in peace with each other. And we urge you, brothers and sisters, warn those who are idle and disruptive, encourage the disheartened, help the weak, be patient with everyone. Make sure that nobody pays back wrong for wrong, but always strive to do what is good for each other and for everyone else. Rejoice always, pray continually, give thanks in all circumstances; for this is God's will for you in Christ Jesus."

1 Thessalonians 5:12-18 NIV

Such encouraging comments as these, never lose their significance. My prayer today is that we would each display such a positive attitude in our witness to those around us!

Bonnie

Bonnie's Blessings

May 19

"Peace I leave with you; my peace I give you. I do not give to you as the world gives. Do not let your hearts be troubled and do not be afraid."

John 14:27 NIV

Beautiful words of comfort that Jesus gave to His disciples as He knew He was about to leave them and go to heaven. How wonderful that He also made a way for you and I to also claim that same Peace! This is precious reassurance, especially as we say "farewell for now" to fellow Christians who have recently been called Home to their eternal reward. Thank You, Lord, for Your Promises!

Bonnie

149.

Bonnie's Blessings

May 20

"To humans belong the plans of the heart, but from the Lord comes the proper answer of the tongue. All a person's ways seem pure to them, but motives are weighed by the Lord. Commit to the Lord whatever you do, and He will establish your plans. The Lord works out everything to its proper end— even the wicked for a day of disaster. The Lord detests all the proud of heart. Be sure of this: They will not go unpunished. Through love and faithfulness sin is atoned for; through the fear of the Lord evil is avoided. When the Lord takes pleasure in anyone's way, he causes their enemies to make peace with them. Better a little with righteousness than much gain with injustice. In their hearts humans plan their course, but the Lord establishes their steps."

Proverbs 16:1-9 NIV

The Book of Proverbs is, of course, filled with words of wisdom which apply to each of us in some way. However, I selected this particular chapter to focus on all the graduates... of many ages!! Our prayer, naturally, should be that each graduate would be seeking wisdom from The Lord as they launch out on their life adventures! Although He does not promise we will always be "wealthy and healthy", still Our God does promise to always be available! Call on Him...and He Will Listen! And He DOES Care!! I know this in my own life... beyond a doubt!! And it is my prayer today that we would each pause to Thank Him for His Blessings! May The Lord Bless you and hold you today in His Everlasting Arms!!   150.   Bonnie

May 21

"Listen to advice and accept discipline, and at the end you will be counted among the wise. Many are the plans in a person's heart, but it is the Lord's purpose that prevails. What a person desires is unfailing love; better to be poor than a liar. The fear of the Lord leads to life; then one rests content, untouched by trouble."

Proverbs 19:20-23 NIV

Focusing my prayers this morning on our graduates... what a special event in life, with feelings of accomplishment, as well as anticipation for whatever is ahead! May God's Love shine brightly today on all who are seeking His Will in their choices and steps, no matter at what stage of life!

Bonnie

May 22

"Jesus said to her, "Your brother will rise again." Martha answered, "I know he will rise again in the resurrection at the last day." Jesus said to her, "I am the resurrection and the life. The one who believes in me will live, even though they die; and whoever lives by believing in me will never die. Do you believe this?" "Yes, Lord," she replied, "I believe that you are the Messiah, the Son of God, who is to come into the world.""

John 11:23-27 NIV

Attending a funeral later today for a friend who had already claimed God's Promises. He also was constantly concerned about those who had not claimed those promises... And even more concerned about those who had not yet heard of the saving Grace available through Christ our Lord. Anyone who had talked with Ben had heard about Jesus! What a precious example for all of us to follow!

Bonnie

May 23

"They devoted themselves to the apostles' teaching and to fellowship, to the breaking of bread and to prayer. Everyone was filled with awe at the many wonders and signs performed by the apostles. All the believers were together and had everything in common. They sold property and possessions to give to anyone who had need. Every day they continued to meet together in the temple courts. They broke bread in their homes and ate together with glad and sincere hearts, praising God and enjoying the favor of all the people. And the Lord added to their number daily those who were being saved."

Acts 2:42-47 NIV

I have always thought how amazing it would have been to be there on that day of Pentecost to witness all that happened, and to worship with that group of believers! Yet even a greater event is ahead, when Christ returns!! And we must spread the Word to be ready!

153.

Bonnie

May 24

"Therefore if you have any encouragement from being united with Christ, if any comfort from his love, if any common sharing in the Spirit, if any tenderness and compassion, then make my joy complete by being like-minded, having the same love, being one in spirit and of one mind. Do nothing out of selfish ambition or vain conceit. Rather, in humility value others above yourselves, not looking to your own interests but each of you to the interests of the others. In your relationships with one another, have the same mindset as Christ Jesus: Who, being in very nature God, did not consider equality with God something to be used to his own advantage; rather, he made himself nothing by taking the very nature of a servant, being made in human likeness. And being found in appearance as a man, he humbled himself by becoming obedient to death— even death on a cross! Therefore God exalted him to the highest place and gave him the name that is above every name, that at the name of Jesus every knee should bow, in heaven and on earth and under the earth, and every tongue acknowledge that Jesus Christ is Lord, to the glory of God the Father."

Philippians 2:1-11 NIV

In my simplistic way of thinking, these verses form a beautiful description of Christianity! Because it's all centered on Christ, and seeking to pattern our lives after Him; it is a blessing and privilege to be His follower. It is a blessing and relief to place my life under HIS Control! THANK YOU, LORD!! 154.

Bonnie

May 25

"Very truly I tell you, whoever believes in me will do the works I have been doing, and they will do even greater things than these, because I am going to the Father. And I will do whatever you ask in my name, so that the Father may be glorified in the Son. You may ask me for anything in my name, and I will do it."

John 14:12-14 NIV

I can recall when I was much younger in the Faith, that I tried to use this passage like a wishlist ("you may ask me for anything")... then someone wiser pointed out the condition "in My name."] Our requests should be mainly for wisdom and strength to carry out His Will while we are here on earth. This does NOT mean that we should hesitate to pray for someone's health, or for needed provisions-- like needed food or shelter--- but we should still strive to focus our lives on serving God and sharing the Good News about Jesus. Amen!!

Bonnie

155.

May 26

""Blessed are the poor in spirit, for theirs is the kingdom of heaven. Blessed are those who mourn, for they will be comforted. Blessed are the meek, for they will inherit the earth. Blessed are those who hunger and thirst for righteousness, for they will be filled. Blessed are the merciful, for they will be shown mercy. Blessed are the pure in heart, for they will see God. Blessed are the peacemakers, for they will be called children of God. Blessed are those who are persecuted because of righteousness, for theirs is the kingdom of heaven."

Matthew 5:3-10 NIV

Precious Words of Jesus, from what we now call "The Sermon on the Mount". Bud and I have such treasured memories of our trip to the Holy Land so many years ago. One day of that journey included sitting on that hillside, while someone read aloud the beautiful Words that are now recorded for us in the Gospels. I am praying that YOU will be blessed by His Truths today!

Bonnie

156.

May 27

"Start children off on the way they should go, and when they are old they will not turn from it."

Proverbs 22:6 NIV

"I will instruct you and teach you in the way you should go; I will counsel you with my loving eye on you."

Psalm 32:8 NIV

— ❖•❖ —

Today, as we honor and thank "Miss Anita" for all her years of teaching at New Horizon Christian School ····. These verses seem appropriate.

We love and admire our wonderful Anita Newlin, and pray she will greatly enjoy her retirement as she continues to let Jesus Shine through her!

Bonnie

163

May 28

"For the word of God is alive and active. Sharper than any double-edged sword, it penetrates even to dividing soul and spirit, joints and marrow; it judges the thoughts and attitudes of the heart. Nothing in all creation is hidden from God's sight. Everything is uncovered and laid bare before the eyes of him to whom we must give account. Therefore, since we have a great high priest who has ascended into heaven, Jesus the Son of God, let us hold firmly to the faith we profess. For we do not have a high priest who is unable to empathize with our weaknesses, but we have one who has been tempted in every way, just as we are—yet he did not sin. Let us then approach God's throne of grace with confidence, so that we may receive mercy and find grace to help us in our time of need."

Hebrews 4:12-16 NIV

It is an awesome realization that our Great God knows my every thought and motive and action! He knows what I have done to serve Him, and He knows what I failed to do... even though I clearly felt Him prompting me to take action! He knows my intentions, and He is merciful and kind. He is a "good good Father!" I run to Him, and He holds me! He comforts me, and gives me peace in the midst of my storm! ... Friend, I trust that you also lean on Him, and look to Him as the "author and sustainer of your life!" This is my prayer today.

Bonnie

May 29

"Very truly I tell you, whoever believes in me will do the works I have been doing, and they will do even greater things than these, because I am going to the Father. And I will do whatever you ask in my name, so that the Father may be glorified in the Son. You may ask me for anything in my name, and I will do it."

John 14:12-14 NIV

I can recall when I was much younger in the Faith, that I tried to use this passage like a wishlist ("you may ask me for anything")... then someone wiser pointed out the condition "in My name."] Our requests should be mainly for wisdom and strength to carry out His Will while we are here on earth. This does NOT mean that we should hesitate to pray for someone's health, or for needed provisions-- like needed food or shelter--- but we should still strive to focus our lives on serving God and sharing the Good News about Jesus. Amen!!

Bonnie

159.

May 30

""Listen then to what the parable of the sower means: When anyone hears the message about the kingdom and does not understand it, the evil one comes and snatches away what was sown in their heart. This is the seed sown along the path. The seed falling on rocky ground refers to someone who hears the word and at once receives it with joy. But since they have no root, they last only a short time. When trouble or persecution comes because of the word, they quickly fall away. The seed falling among the thorns refers to someone who hears the word, but the worries of this life and the deceitfulness of wealth choke the word, making it unfruitful. But the seed falling on good soil refers to someone who hears the word and understands it. This is the one who produces a crop, yielding a hundred, sixty or thirty times what was sown.""

Matthew 13:18-23 NIV

Last night Bud and our son John were so grateful for the rain. Being married to a farmer, I am fascinated by the truths revealed in the Parables that Jesus told regarding seed time and harvest. God has a plan, and He intends for us to be a part of His Plan... sowing the Seed of His Word... and helping to nurture the soil... looking forward to The Harvest! We need to each be eager to do our part working in His fields.   160.

Bonnie

May 31

This morning, I "started on the wrong foot"... frustrated by all my silly mistakes and frequent "forgetfulness", which accompany my current physical status (which includes what they call "short-term memory loss.") ... So I offered all this up to The Lord, as I frequently do, and here are some of the refreshing answers He gave me today. ...

"Blessed are those who acclaim You, who walk in the light of Your presence, Lord."

Psalm 89:15 NIV

"Give thanks to The Lord, for He is good; His Love endures forever!"

Psalm 118:1 NIV

"...always giving thanks to the God the Father for everything, in the name of Jesus our Lord."

Ephesians 5:20 NIV

So, now I am ready to face this new day, trusting in Him, "No Matter What!" ... Praying that YOU have a blessed day!!

Bonnie

June

Bonnie's Blessings

June 1

"Shout for joy to the Lord, all the earth. Worship the Lord with gladness; come before him with joyful songs. Know that the Lord is God. It is he who made us, and we are his; we are his people, the sheep of his pasture. Enter his gates with thanksgiving and his courts with praise; give thanks to him and praise his name. For the Lord is good and his love endures forever; his faithfulness continues through all generations."

Psalms 100:1-5 NIV

Even as a child, I always looked forward to Sunday mornings... I have no clear memories of any preacher but "my Daddy" as a young child... and he is the one who baptized me at the age of 8. Then in Korea (my 5th thru 8th grade) we worshipped at various churches...sometimes Dad was the preacher, with an interpreter... women sitting on floor on one side; men on the other side. Back then I could sing many of the hymns and choruses in Korean, but now I can only do that if reading from the hymnal! When we returned to the States, my faith grew even more, and so did my love of songs of worship. That is only one form of worship... but it totally thrills my heart! How about you?] I am so ready to worship in His House with others today! Give Him Thanks and Praise His Name!!

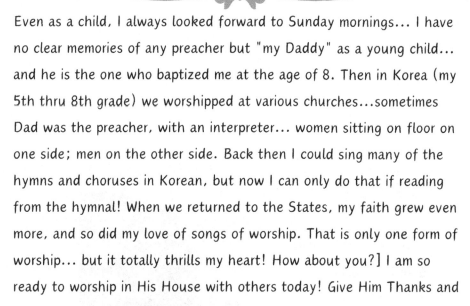

163.

Bonnie

June 2

"Be patient, then, brothers and sisters, until the Lord's coming. See how the farmer waits for the land to yield its valuable crop, patiently waiting for the autumn and spring rains. You too, be patient and stand firm, because the Lord's coming is near."

James 5:7-8 NIV

———— ✦·✦ ————

As I have mentioned before, James is my favorite Epistle---so full of wisdom. I focus on these verses often, for two reasons: (1) I love My Farmer Bud, and his passion for farming, and his dependence on God to supply what is needed... (2) Because I need this reminder to NOT "grumble and complain" ... but rather to have "patience in the face of suffering" ... These thoughts apply to EVERYONE at some point in their life journey. Lean on Jesus, and He Will Walk Beside You!

Harvest time ride with
Grandpa Klockenga
2009.

Bonnie

June 2

"Therefore, since we are surrounded by such a great cloud of witnesses, let us throw off everything that hinders and the sin that so easily entangles. And let us run with perseverance the race marked out for us, fixing our eyes on Jesus, the pioneer and perfecter of faith. For the joy set before him he endured the cross, scorning its shame, and sat down at the right hand of the throne of God. Consider him who endured such opposition from sinners, so that you will not grow weary and lose heart."

Hebrews 12:1-3 NIV

This morning, as I was reading various devotionals, and favorite Scripture passages, I was considering what to share with you today. Naturally my mind is on the many graduates this month --- we have several in our own family circle!-- and I was quickly drawn to this well-known passage. I hope it will "spur you on" today! Bonnie

165.

June 3

"Devote yourselves to prayer, being watchful and thankful. And pray for us, too, that God may open a door for our message, so that we may proclaim the mystery of Christ, for which I am in chains. Pray that I may proclaim it clearly, as I should. Be wise in the way you act toward outsiders; make the most of every opportunity. Let your conversation be always full of grace, seasoned with salt, so that you may know how to answer everyone."

Colossians 4:2-6 NIV.

It is interesting to note here that the great Apostle Paul puts great emphasis on the importance of prayer.... whether you are praying for a missionary overseas, or praying about your own heart and attitude; God is listening! These verses also refer to our attitudes and conversations around others. People around us are watching and listening too! Each one of us can be "a sermon in shoes!"

Bonnie

June 4

"Show me your ways, Lord, teach me your paths. Guide me in your truth and teach me, for you are God my Savior, and my hope is in you all day long. Remember, Lord, your great mercy and love, for they are from of old. Do not remember the sins of my youth and my rebellious ways; according to your love remember me, for you, Lord, are good."

Psalms 25:4-7 NIV

Trying to lean more faithfully on Our Lord for guidance and wisdom and strength in each choice that I make... whether it is in how I spend my time and energy... or how I take care of my body and our house... or how I treat the people God has placed in my life. I long to be more accountable to My Lord in how I make good use of the countless blessings He has placed in my life. And if you are reading this message, please know that I consider YOU as one of those blessings. Our God is Good... All the Time!

167.

Bonnie

June 5

"Consider it pure joy, my brothers and sisters, whenever you face trials of many kinds, because you know that the testing of your faith produces perseverance. Let perseverance finish its work so that you may be mature and complete, not lacking anything. If any of you lacks wisdom, you should ask God, who gives generously to all without finding fault, and it will be given to you."

James 1:2-5 NIV

At every stage of life, or times of challenging choices, the words in these verses provide perfect guidance: "Ask God." Absolutely as graduation time comes around each year, I turn to this passage. Let's encourage our graduates to put God first in all their plans and decisions that are ahead. AND the rest of us should do the same with any choices, big or small! Then, as we are leaning on Him... let's take this advice to heart: "Consider it pure joy!"

Bonnie

168.

June 6

"Three times I pleaded with the Lord to take it away from me. But he said to me, "My grace is sufficient for you, for my power is made perfect in weakness." Therefore I will boast all the more gladly about my weaknesses, so that Christ's power may rest on me. That is why, for Christ's sake, I delight in weaknesses, in insults, in hardships, in persecutions, in difficulties. For when I am weak, then I am strong."

2 Corinthians 12:8-10 NIV

At great risk of being misunderstood, I want to share with you that these verses spoke directly to my own heart today! Most of you who receive verses from me daily know that I am going through some very real struggles that directly affect my memory... at times I struggle to even recall what YEAR this is, let alone what I planned to fix for supper tonight... but in the midst of all my confusion, God's Word ALWAYS gives me such Peace and Reassurance, that Our God Reigns... and He Knows My Name!! He will guide me through ANY Storm! And ultimately He will greet me on the Other Shore!! But Until Then... My Heart Will Keep On Singing!! And life is full of love and peace and happiness! I pray the same assurance for YOU.... No Matter What!!] With Love and Prayers,

Bonnie

These beautiful daughters of mine bless my life daily!!

June 7

"Do not fret because of those who are evil or be envious of those who do wrong; for like the grass they will soon wither, like green plants they will soon die away. Trust in the Lord and do good; dwell in the land and enjoy safe pasture. Take delight in the Lord, and he will give you the desires of your heart. Commit your way to the Lord; trust in him and he will do this: He will make your righteous reward shine like the dawn, your vindication like the noonday sun. Be still before the Lord and wait patiently for him; do not fret when people succeed in their ways, when they carry out their wicked schemes. Refrain from anger and turn from wrath; do not fret—it leads only to evil. For those who are evil will be destroyed, but those who hope in the Lord will inherit the land. A little while, and the wicked will be no more; though you look for them, they will not be found. But the meek will inherit the land and enjoy peace and prosperity."

Psalms 37:1-11 NIV

These thoughts remind me of the song "It Will Be Worth It All when We See Jesus!".... The THINGS of this world cannot possibly compare to the peace and contentment of living for The Lord. Let's agree to "not fret" today! Simply "delight in the Lord!"... and read the rest of Psalm 37!

Bonnie

June 8

"This is what I have observed to be good: that it is appropriate for a person to eat, to drink and to find satisfaction in their toilsome labor under the sun during the few days of life God has given them—for this is their lot. Moreover, when God gives someone wealth and possessions, and the ability to enjoy them, to accept their lot and be happy in their toil—this is a gift of God. They seldom reflect on the days of their life, because God keeps them occupied with gladness of heart."

Ecclesiastes 5:18-20 NIV

And here is my simple personal application of these words of wisdom:

"It's all about attitude!! When we look for the GOOD in all The Lord provides, and eagerly SHARE The Good News, our life is full of purpose and anticipation for even better things to come··· throughout Eternity!! HE IS LORD of my life, so Each Day Counts!] Praying YOU feel Blessed Today!

Bonnie

June 9

"But as for me, I watch in hope for the Lord, I wait for God my Savior; my God will hear me."

Micah 7:7 NIV

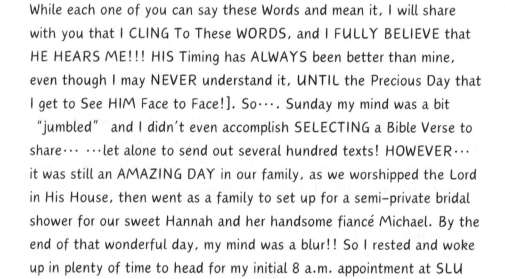

While each one of you can say these Words and mean it, I will share with you that I CLING To These WORDS, and I FULLY BELIEVE that HE HEARS ME!!! HIS Timing has ALWAYS been better than mine, even though I may NEVER understand it, UNTIL the Precious Day that I get to See HIM Face to Face!]. So···. Sunday my mind was a bit "jumbled" and I didn't even accomplish SELECTING a Bible Verse to share··· ···let alone to send out several hundred texts! HOWEVER··· it was still an AMAZING DAY in our family, as we worshipped the Lord in His House, then went as a family to set up for a semi-private bridal shower for our sweet Hannah and her handsome fiancé Michael. By the end of that wonderful day, my mind was a blur!! So I rested and woke up in plenty of time to head for my initial 8 a.m. appointment at SLU Memory Clinic. JUST before we arrived there today, Bud received call on his cell phone that the Doctor was ill, and our appointment would need to be rescheduled! While we were disappointed, this is NOT an emergency and it has already been rescheduled for August. That's not a terribly long wait since I am NOT feeling ill or in pain. We continue to trust Our Lord to walk beside us. THANKS So Much for your prayers and concern. Together We Will "Watch and Hope!"

Bonnie

172.

June 10

"These are the commands, decrees and laws the Lord your God directed me to teach you to observe in the land that you are crossing the Jordan to possess, so that you, your children and their children after them may fear the Lord your God as long as you live by keeping all his decrees and commands that I give you, and so that you may enjoy long life. Hear, Israel, and be careful to obey so that it may go well with you and that you may increase greatly in a land flowing with milk and honey, just as the Lord, the God of your ancestors, promised you. Hear, O Israel: The Lord our God, the Lord is one. Love the Lord your God with all your heart and with all your soul and with all your strength. These commandments that I give you today are to be on your hearts. Impress them on your children. Talk about them when you sit at home and when you walk along the road, when you lie down and when you get up. Tie them as symbols on your hands and bind them on your foreheads. Write them on the doorframes of your houses and on your gates."

Deuteronomy 6:1-9 NIV

Studying and Sharing God's Word is to be our daily focus!

Bonnie

June 11

"And this is my prayer: that your love may abound more and more in knowledge and depth of insight, so that you may be able to discern what is best and may be pure and blameless for the day of Christ, filled with the fruit of righteousness that comes through Jesus Christ—to the glory and praise of God."

Philippians 1:9-11 NIV

If you truly know me, then you are aware that I actually have a pretty simplistic outlook on life!]... I am extremely blessed by the family and friends that surround me... and most of all by the Love and Salvation that I receive through Jesus Christ my Lord. The AMAZING thing too, is that this same joy, and peace in the midst of trials, is AVAILABLE TO EVERYONE!! Our main focus literally needs to be to display and SHARE that GOOD NEWS with EVERYONE we meet. *Bonnie*

174.

June 12

I remain confident of this: I will see the goodness of the Lord in the land of the living. Wait for the Lord; be strong and take heart and wait for the Lord."

Psalms 27:13-14 NIV

———— ✦•✦ ————

No matter where your path leads you today, these Words are a great reminder to "Wait for the Lord, be strong and take heart and wait for the Lord." ···. HE Himself is the answer ···. ALWAYS!! And HE gives me a peaceful heart. *Bonnie*

175.

June 13

"Listen, you heavens, and I will speak; hear, you earth, the words of my mouth. Let my teaching fall like rain and my words descend like dew, like showers on new grass, like abundant rain on tender plants. I will proclaim the name of the Lord. Oh, praise the greatness of our God! He is the Rock, his works are perfect, and all his ways are just. A faithful God who does no wrong, upright and just is he."

Deuteronomy 32:1-4 NIV

It is so pleasant on a morning like this to just relax with my coffee and devotions time··· be in His Word··· watching and listening as the rain is falling. Granted, I recall the days when I still needed to hurry off to work, regardless of the weather! But my point is that through it all, HE is Faithful and provides for our needs··· and much more besides! So let's give Him Praise today!! *Bonnie*

June 14

"Who is wise and understanding among you? Let them show it by their good life, by deeds done in the humility that comes from wisdom. But if you harbor bitter envy and selfish ambition in your hearts, do not boast about it or deny the truth. Such "wisdom" does not come down from heaven but is earthly, unspiritual, demonic. For where you have envy and selfish ambition, there you find disorder and every evil practice. But the wisdom that comes from heaven is first of all pure; then peace-loving, considerate, submissive, full of mercy and good fruit, impartial and sincere. Peacemakers who sow in peace reap a harvest of righteousness."

James 3:13-18 NIV

All through James' letter, he is making thought-provoking comparisons. I want to be a wise peacemaker! How about you?!? But that takes a lot of patience and growth... I have a lot more "growing" to do, and I am often short on patience! Let's agree to pray for each other to grow in this area.

Bonnie

June 15

"Jesus said to her, "Your brother will rise again." Martha answered, "I know he will rise again in the resurrection at the last day." Jesus said to her, "I am the resurrection and the life. The one who believes in me will live, even though they die; and whoever lives by believing in me will never die. Do you believe this?" "Yes, Lord," she replied, "I believe that you are the Messiah, the Son of God, who is to come into the world.""

John 11:23-27 NIV

———— ◆·◆ ————

Praise the Lord that we have this same Hope! I too believe that Jesus is the Messiah, the Son of God!

Bonnie

June 16

"Do you not know that your bodies are temples of the Holy Spirit, who is in you, whom you have received from God? You are not your own; you were bought at a price. Therefore honor God with your bodies." 1 Corinthians 6:19-20 NIV [This is very personal, I am aware... but I want to be held accountable and encouraged to take better care of this body God has given me!! The area I struggle with is in eating properly and exercising... that's where I am lax. And I DO want to "honor God with my body" by taking better care of it. I share these very personal thoughts intentionally because I hope that we can ALL be more aware that we are literally moving around here on earth in a "temple of the Holy Spirit"!!! And we need to handle it with Respect! This is NOT always an easy assignment! Let's please agree to "Honor God with our bodies!"

1 Corinthians 6:19-20 NIV

This is very personal, I am aware... but I want to be held accountable and encouraged to take better care of this body God has given me!! The area I struggle with is in eating properly and exercising... that's where I am lax. And I DO want to "honor God with my body" by taking better care of it. I share these very personal thoughts intentionally because I hope that we can ALL be more aware that we are literally moving around here on earth in a "temple of the Holy Spirit"!!! And we need to handle it with Respect! This is NOT always an easy assignment! Let's please agree to "Honor God with our bodies!"

179.

Bonnie

June 17

"Love is patient, love is kind. It does not envy, it does not boast, it is not proud. It does not dishonor others, it is not self-seeking, it is not easily angered, it keeps no record of wrongs. Love does not delight in evil but rejoices with the truth. It always protects, always trusts, always hopes, always perseveres. Love never fails. But where there are prophecies, they will cease; where there are tongues, they will be stilled; where there is knowledge, it will pass away. For we know in part and we prophesy in part, but when completeness comes, what is in part disappears. When I was a child, I talked like a child, I thought like a child, I reasoned like a child. When I became a man, I put the ways of childhood behind me. For now we see only a reflection as in a mirror; then we shall see face to face. Now I know in part; then I shall know fully, even as I am fully known. And now these three remain: faith, hope and love. But the greatest of these is love."

1 Corinthians 13:4-13 NIV

It is so good to focus on LOVE··· Especially the Love of God. HE is amazing, and HE deserves our Love and Adoration!! It is a simple truth that when I focus my mind on Loving God, and sharing His Love with others, the day is brighter··· No Matter What else is happening in my life!! Our God is So Good··· All the Time!!

Bonnie

180.

June 18

"As a father has compassion on his children, so the Lord has compassion on those who fear him; for he knows how we are formed, he remembers that we are dust. The life of mortals is like grass, they flourish like a flower of the field; the wind blows over it and it is gone, and its place remembers it no more. But from everlasting to everlasting the Lord's love is with those who fear him, and his righteousness with their children's children— with those who keep his covenant and remember to obey his precepts."

Psalms 103:13-18 NIV

How blessed are those of us who have a Christian father who demonstrates love and compassion··· yet even those who are not so blessed are still welcomed into the arms of a loving Heavenly Father.

Bonnie

June 19

"Finally, be strong in the Lord and in his mighty power. Put on the full armor of God, so that you can take your stand against the devil's schemes. For our struggle is not against flesh and blood, but against the rulers, against the authorities, against the powers of this dark world and against the spiritual forces of evil in the heavenly realms. Therefore put on the full armor of God, so that when the day of evil comes, you may be able to stand your ground, and after you have done everything, to stand. Stand firm then, with the belt of truth buckled around your waist, with the breastplate of righteousness in place, and with your feet fitted with the readiness that comes from the gospel of peace. In addition to all this, take up the shield of faith, with which you can extinguish all the flaming arrows of the evil one. Take the helmet of salvation and the sword of the Spirit, which is the word of God. And pray in the Spirit on all occasions with all kinds of prayers and requests. With this in mind, be alert and always keep on praying for all the Lord's people. Pray also for me, that whenever I speak, words may be given me so that I will fearlessly make known the mystery of the gospel, for which I am an ambassador in chains. Pray that I may declare it fearlessly, as I should."

Ephesians 6:10-20 NIV

If the early Christians needed to pray for each other to be strong in their faith, how much more so do we today need to be praying for, and encouraging each other to stand firm!?!] Before I sent this today, I prayed for you by name. With My Love and Prayers, *Bonnie*

June 20

"What, then, shall we say in response to these things? If God is for us, who can be against us? He who did not spare his own Son, but gave him up for us all—how will he not also, along with him, graciously give us all things? Who will bring any charge against those whom God has chosen? It is God who justifies. Who then is the one who condemns? No one. Christ Jesus who died—more than that, who was raised to life—is at the right hand of God and is also interceding for us. Who shall separate us from the love of Christ? Shall trouble or hardship or persecution or famine or nakedness or danger or sword? As it is written: "For your sake we face death all day long; we are considered as sheep to be slaughtered." No, in all these things we are more than conquerors through him who loved us. For I am convinced that neither death nor life, neither angels nor demons, neither the present nor the future, nor any powers, neither height nor depth, nor anything else in all creation, will be able to separate us from the love of God that is in Christ Jesus our Lord."

Romans 8:31-39 NIV

———— ✦·✦ ————

Such a powerful declaration of the hope God gives us, in any situation! Jesus Is The Answer!

Bonnie

Grandma's Vacation Scavenger Hunt

Grandma's Scavenger Hunt. (The grandkids get 10 cents for each item they complete and each State license plate they see.) Then whoever wins the most each year gets to select a mission...and each of his cousins may donate a portion of their winnings if they choose to.

June 21

"He replied, "Because you have so little faith. Truly I tell you, if you have faith as small as a mustard seed, you can say to this mountain, 'Move from here to there,' and it will move. Nothing will be impossible for you.""

Matthew 17:20 NIV

——— ◆·◆ ———

Currently I am struggling (Again!) with overcoming my weight problem··· and I am so dependent on my Lord to help me!! In my life, one of my mountains is being overweight, because it is unhealthy and that prevents me from being as active as I want and need to be. Each of us need to identify our mountains ··· name them··· pray for God's help to conquer them··· ask others to encourage us. That's what I am doing today. My problem is obvious to anyone who sees me. It may be nice to hear "you look fine to me" but in fact I need encouragement to focus right now on a healthier lifestyle so that I can be more active and keep on serving our great Father!] I hope this personal note can encourage you to recognize that we all need to rely on each other, and most of all on Our Lord, in order to be at our best, and to serve Him well! With My Love n Prayers,   185   *Bonnie*

June 22

"Search me, God, and know my heart; test me and know my anxious thoughts. See if there is any offensive way in me, and lead me in the way everlasting."

Psalms 139:23-24 NIV

During my morning devotions, part of the time, I read various Devotionals··· I often select one, then read the whole week instead of rushing thru just one-day devotional····. Because I CAN··· I am Retired!··· Anyway, Day 6 of the 7-day series I read today included this comment about verses 23-24, and it hit me right where I am right now!! [The following are NOT my words··· I am quoting:] "Who we become is directly impacted by our thoughts because our thoughts become our decisions and behaviors. That's why today's verses matter··· Becoming who God wants us to be starts with changing our thinking. This is what Jesus meant when He said to Repent. It's our invitation to turn away from negative thoughts and behaviors, and to change how we THINK! Regarding our view of ourselves and our bodies, we need to "Repent and change our THINKING!" So, the question is: Where do you need to "Repent" regarding how you think about yourself and your body? Ask God to search your heart and "Lead you into the way everlasting" ····.. [Ok, there you have it··· I have a LOT of thinking and praying and adjusting to do. And I hope YOU have a blessed day yourself, leaning on Our God to show you the way! 186. *Bonnie*

June 23

"To him who is able to keep you from stumbling and to present you before his glorious presence without fault and with great joy— to the only God our Savior be glory, majesty, power and authority, through Jesus Christ our Lord, before all ages, now and forevermore! Amen."

Jude 1:24-25 NIV

Let us praise Him today, with the words we speak, and by our actions!!

Bonnie

June 24

"Do not be deceived: God cannot be mocked. A man reaps what he sows. Whoever sows to please their flesh, from the flesh will reap destruction; whoever sows to please the Spirit, from the Spirit will reap eternal life. Let us not become weary in doing good, for at the proper time we will reap a harvest if we do not give up. Therefore, as we have opportunity, let us do good to all people, especially to those who belong to the family of believers."

Galatians 6:7-10 NIV

These verses came up in my Scripture reading this morning, at the same time that we are thanking God for the best wheat harvest ever on our farm··· and it is a reminder that the most important harvest comes when we can rejoice over the hearts and souls that are gathered at the Throne! When men and women, boys and girls, declare that Jesus is The Christ, the Son of God—– and they accept Him as Lord of their life, and are obedient in baptism, according to The Scriptures! There is much more rejoicing in Heaven over that precious harvest!! Thank You, Lord!!

Bonnie

June 25

"Let the morning bring me word of your unfailing love, for I have put my trust in you. Show me the way I should go, for to you I lift up my soul."

Psalm 143:8 NIV

Actual photo this morning as I began my devotion time on the deck.

Feeling extremely blessed, as I read God's Word to start the day.

Praying your day is filled with gratitude, and joy in Serving Jesus today,

through your thoughts, words, and actions!

Bonnie

June 26

"My son, do not forget my teaching, but keep my commands in your heart, for they will prolong your life many years and bring you peace and prosperity. Let love and faithfulness never leave you; bind them around your neck, write them on the tablet of your heart. Then you will win favor and a good name in the sight of God and man. Trust in the Lord with all your heart and lean not on your own understanding; in all your ways submit to him, and he will make your paths straight. Do not be wise in your own eyes; fear the Lord and shun evil. This will bring health to your body and nourishment to your bones. Honor the Lord with your wealth, with the firstfruits of all your crops; then your barns will be filled to overflowing, and your vats will brim over with new wine. My son, do not despise the Lord's discipline, and do not resent his rebuke, because the Lord disciplines those he loves, as a father the son he delights in."

Proverbs 3:1-12 NIV

Praying that we will each "Trust in the Lord" for every choice and decision we will face in the days ahead this week. He stands ready to guide and bless us!

190.

Bonnie

Bonnie's Blessings

June 27

"Remind the people to be subject to rulers and authorities, to be obedient, to be ready to do whatever is good, to slander no one, to be peaceable and considerate, and always to be gentle toward everyone."

Titus 3:1-2 NIV

— ❖·❖ —

Such advice in Scripture certainly emphasizes the need to be responsible citizens wherever we live. In America, it seems so easy to express our own opinions, but if we are not responsible enough to "do our part" then we really are neglecting some of our opportunities to have a positive influence in our nation and community. My True Freedom is in Christ!! Now, while serving Him, in my life I want to strive to live and act in an appropriate respectful manner.

Bonnie

191.

June 28

"I know what it is to be in need, and I know what it is to have plenty. I have learned the secret of being content in any and every situation, whether well fed or hungry, whether living in plenty or in want. I can do all this through him who gives me strength."

Philippians 4:12-13 NIV.

Although these verses are not about dieting, The Lord has definitely been helping me to stay focused on my eating plan··· in this first 8 days I have now lost 8.4 pounds!··· I got a good scale that shows your weight and % water etc.

Bonnie

June 29

"Discipline your children, and they will give you peace; they will bring you the delights you desire. Where there is no revelation, people cast off restraint; but blessed is the one who heeds wisdom's instruction."

Proverbs 29:17-18 NIV

Good Morning! Today is the 29th··· a simple reminder to read the 29th chapter of Proverbs! God's Word never fails to inspire and challenge me to do better! God is so Good! All the time!!]··· ALSO Please be praying for safe travels for the George Family returning to India.

Bonnie

This picture was taken in 2018 when Bud and Bonnie went to India to visit the George's and the House of Hope Orphanage.

193.

June 30

"Ask and it will be given to you. Seek and you will find. Knock and the door will be open to you."

Matthew 7:7 NIV

"Come near to God and He will come near to you."

James 4:8 NIV

This week one of the devotionals I am reading is "Hymn of Heaven: A 12-Day Devotional with Phil Wickman" [This also led me to his song "Falling in Love" which includes these lyrics: "The more I praise You, the more I want to. I'm falling in love, falling in love with You. I lay my life down. God, I am Yours now. I'm falling in love, falling in love with You."]

Bonnie

July 1

July 1

"The Lord has done great things for us, and we are filled with joy."

Psalms 126:3 NIV

Hopefully, you have had days when you have been "filled with joy!" I can, with much gratitude, say that I have had many such days throughout my life. On my own calendar, THIS is definitely one such day in my memory bank.] And yet, nothing here on earth can totally compare to the Amazing Gift of our Salvation through Jesus Christ! The truth of that Gift is profound!!! As excited as I get sharing the stories of the joyful events of each our children being born····. How much GREATER and more POWERFUL is the AMAZING NEWS that Christ came to earth to deliver Peace and Salvation to each of us. We MUST be excited about that Amazing Miraculous Good News!! Let's Praise Him today!! "He has done great things for us!"

Bonnie

Have you heard one of my favorite true stories???

Long before sonograms were a common practice, the doctor didn't even hear two heartbeats until a little before Jennifer was born····. Then the doctor announced "Here comes another one··· Get that man a chair!" [Bud did not sit down]······ and 6 minutes later John arrived!

July 2

And he said, "These are they who have come out of the
great tribulation; they have washed their robes and made
them white in the blood of the Lamb. Therefore, "they are
before the throne of God and serve him day and night in
his temple; and he who sits on the throne will shelter them
with his presence. 'Never again will they hunger; never
again will they thirst. The sun will not beat down on them,'
nor any scorching heat. For the Lamb at the center of the
throne will be their shepherd; 'he will lead them to springs
of living water.' 'And God will wipe away every tear from
their eyes.'""

Revelation 7:14-17 NIV

While I am privileged to serve and praise Our Lord here, I am
also eager to praise Him around His Throne, for all eternity!
Not because I have earned the privilege, but because I have
been "washed in the blood of The Lamb!"

Bonnie

July 3

"I waited patiently for the Lord; he turned to me and heard my cry. He lifted me out of the slimy pit, out of the mud and mire; he set my feet on a rock and gave me a firm place to stand. He put a new song in my mouth, a hymn of praise to our God. Many will see and fear the Lord and put their trust in him. Blessed is the one who trusts in the Lord, who does not look to the proud, to those who turn aside to false gods. Many, Lord my God, are the wonders you have done, the things you planned for us. None can compare with you; were I to speak and tell of your deeds, they would be too many to declare. Sacrifice and offering you did not desire— but my ears you have opened— burnt offerings and sin offerings you did not require. Then I said, "Here I am, I have come— it is written about me in the scroll. I desire to do your will, my God; your law is within my heart." I proclaim your saving acts in the great assembly; I do not seal my lips, Lord, as you know. I do not hide your righteousness in my heart; I speak of your faithfulness and your saving help. I do not conceal your love and your faithfulness from the great assembly. Do not withhold your mercy from me, Lord; may your love and faithfulness always protect me."

Psalms 40:1-11 NIV

May Our God be praised today throughout the whole earth!!

Bonnie

Bonnie's Blessings

"Praise the Lord. Praise the Lord, my soul. I will praise the Lord all my life; I will sing praise to my God as long as I live. Do not put your trust in princes, in human beings, who cannot save. When their spirit departs, they return to the ground; on that very day their plans come to nothing. Blessed are those whose help is the God of Jacob, whose hope is in the Lord their God. He is the Maker of heaven and earth, the sea, and everything in them— he remains faithful forever. He upholds the cause of the oppressed and gives food to the hungry. The Lord sets prisoners free, the Lord gives sight to the blind, the Lord lifts up those who are bowed down, the Lord loves the righteous. The Lord watches over the foreigner and sustains the fatherless and the widow, but he frustrates the ways of the wicked. The Lord reigns forever, your God, O Zion, for all generations. Praise the Lord."

Psalms 146:1-10 NIV

Praying that you are doing well. It looks like a pretty sunny day here "down on the farm!"

Bonnie

July 5

"Keep your lives free from the love of money and be content with what you have, because God has said, "Never will I leave you; never will I forsake you." So we say with confidence, "The Lord is my helper; I will not be afraid. What can mere mortals do to me?" Remember your leaders, who spoke the word of God to you. Consider the outcome of their way of life and imitate their faith. Jesus Christ is the same yesterday and today and forever."

Hebrews 13:5-8 NIV

As I read His Word, I am always amazed at the practical advice that is included, which we should apply to our everyday lives! God is so good! We can praise Him with our actions as well as our words!

Bonnie

July 6

"The Lord is my shepherd, I lack nothing. He makes me lie down in green pastures, he leads me beside quiet waters, he refreshes my soul. He guides me along the right paths for his name's sake. Even though I walk through the darkest valley, I will fear no evil, for you are with me; your rod and your staff, they comfort me. You prepare a table before me in the presence of my enemies. You anoint my head with oil; my cup overflows. Surely your goodness and love will follow me all the days of my life, and I will dwell in the house of the Lord forever."

Psalms 23:1-6 NIV

Somehow I never get tired of these precious verses! Praying you feel His Peace and Guidance today!

201.

Bonnie

July 7

"Let love and faithfulness never leave you; bind them around your neck, write them on the tablet of your heart. Then you will win favor and a good name in the sight of God and man."

Proverbs 3:3-4 NIV

This precious Proverb reminds me of a very good caring Christian man in my life, who had a twinkle in his blue eyes when he smiled! Bud's dad, Wendell Charles Klockenga, Sr would have been 103 today.('21) Precious memories.

Bonnie

July 8

"Love must be sincere. Hate what is evil; cling to what is good. Be devoted to one another in love. Honor one another above yourselves. Never be lacking in zeal, but keep your spiritual fervor, serving the Lord. Be joyful in hope, patient in affliction, faithful in prayer. Share with the Lord's people who are in need. Practice hospitality. Bless those who persecute you; bless and do not curse. Rejoice with those who rejoice; mourn with those who mourn. Live in harmony with one another. Do not be proud, but be willing to associate with people of low position. Do not be conceited. Do not repay anyone evil for evil. Be careful to do what is right in the eyes of everyone. If it is possible, as far as it depends on you, live at peace with everyone."

Romans 12:9-18 NIV

✦·✦

WOW! That's a BIG assignment! But it's exactly how we should all aim to live!! So, I need to get busy!! How about you??

Bonnie

July 9

"Rejoice in the Lord always. I will say it again: Rejoice! Let your gentleness be evident to all. The Lord is near. Do not be anxious about anything, but in every situation, by prayer and petition, with thanksgiving, present your requests to God. And the peace of God, which transcends all understanding, will guard your hearts and your minds in Christ Jesus. Finally, brothers and sisters, whatever is true, whatever is noble, whatever is right, whatever is pure, whatever is lovely, whatever is admirable—if anything is excellent or praiseworthy—think about such things."

Philippians 4:4-8 NIV

What a beautiful goal for every day! Indeed—— for every life!!··· I need to keep repeating the statement "Let your gentleness be evident to all" ··· because that is not always the case!! Believe me··· it is worth your time to read this whole chapter··· or even continue and read this whole epistle! And have a great weekend!

204.

Bonnie

July 10

"Praise the Lord. Praise the Lord, you his servants; praise the name of the Lord. Let the name of the Lord be praised, both now and forevermore. From the rising of the sun to the place where it sets, the name of the Lord is to be praised. The Lord is exalted over all the nations, his glory above the heavens. Who is like the Lord our God, the One who sits enthroned on high, who stoops down to look on the heavens and the earth?"

Psalms 113:1-6 NIV

Headed to Branson for a vacation week with all of our children and most of our grandchildren... some had other commitments... all traveling at various times from various directions! Bud and I are stopping at Harvester for church services then traveling rest of the way. Enjoying God's creation and the blessings of family. Praying each of you are feeling blessed today also

Bonnie

July 11

"Therefore, since we are surrounded by such a great cloud of witnesses, let us throw off everything that hinders and the sin that so easily entangles. And let us run with perseverance the race marked out for us, fixing our eyes on Jesus, the pioneer and perfecter of faith. For the joy set before him he endured the cross, scorning its shame, and sat down at the right hand of the throne of God. Consider him who endured such opposition from sinners, so that you will not grow weary and lose heart."

Hebrews 12:1-3 NIV

These verses are even more encouraging when you first read chapter 11, with the list of faithful saints who have endured hardships. Let us "not grow weary and lose heart!" Instead, let's encourage each other to serve the Lord with gladness, spreading the Good News of His Love and Salvation!

206.

Bonnie

July 12

"How can a young person live a clean life? By carefully reading the map of your Word. I'm single-minded in pursuit of you; don't let me miss the road signs you've posted. I've banked your promises in the vault of my heart so I won't sin myself bankrupt. Be blessed, God; train me in your ways of wise living. I'll transfer to my lips all the counsel that comes from your mouth; I delight far more in what you tell me about living than in gathering a pile of riches. I ponder every morsel of wisdom from you, I attentively watch how you've done it. I relish everything you've told me of life, I won't forget a word of it. Be generous with me and I'll live a full life; not for a minute will I take my eyes off your road. Open my eyes so I can see what you show me of your miracle wonders. I'm a stranger in these parts; give me clear directions. My soul is starved and hungry, ravenous!— insatiable for your nourishing commands."

Psalms 119:9:19 MSG

These verses are even more encouraging when you first read chapter 11, with the list of faithful saints who have endured hardships. Let us "not grow weary and lose heart!" Instead, let's encourage each other to serve the Lord with gladness, spreading the Good News of His Love and Salvation!

207.

Bonnie

July 13

"Therefore, since we are surrounded by such a great cloud of witnesses, let us throw off everything that hinders and the sin that so easily entangles. And let us run with perseverance the race marked out for us, fixing our eyes on Jesus, the pioneer and perfecter of faith. For the joy set before him he endured the cross, scorning its shame, and sat down at the right hand of the throne of God. Consider him who endured such opposition from sinners, so that you will not grow weary and lose heart."

Hebrews 12:1-3 NIV

In my life I have ALWAYS been "surrounded by such a great cloud of witnesses" and fir that I am thankful. Today I am reminded that most of the people in this world have never had that privilege or exposure·····praying that we all would be more eager to share the Good News than we ever have before!

Bonnie

208.

Bonnie's Blessings

July 14

"So let's do it—full of belief, confident that we're presentable inside and out. Let's keep a firm grip on the promises that keep us going. He always keeps his word. Let's see how inventive we can be in encouraging love and helping out, not avoiding worshiping together as some do but spurring each other on, especially as we see the big Day approaching."

Hebrews 10:22-25 MSG

Last nite, our GCC Ladies were living out these verses, with a special fellowship time around the pool at Theresa's house... Food, Fun, Fellowship... and great Encouragement from God's Word, led by Frankie Brothers. Doesn't get much better than that!

Bonnie

July 15

"Do not be deceived: God cannot be mocked. A man reaps what he sows. Whoever sows to please their flesh, from the flesh will reap destruction; whoever sows to please the Spirit, from the Spirit will reap eternal life. Let us not become weary in doing good, for at the proper time we will reap a harvest if we do not give up. Therefore, as we have opportunity, let us do good to all people, especially to those who belong to the family of believers."

Galatians 6:7-10 NIV

I have always found Paul's letter to the Galatians to be very practical, with advice that certainly can be applied to my own life. These verses are very plainly talking about how God wants us to treat others.....
"Do good to all people, especially to those who belong to the family of believers." ... I am so very grateful to be a part of that family! How about you?

Bonnie

July 16

"Do not be deceived: God cannot be mocked. A man reaps what he sows. Whoever sows to please their flesh, from the flesh will reap destruction; whoever sows to please the Spirit, from the Spirit will reap eternal life. Let us not become weary in doing good, for at the proper time we will reap a harvest if we do not give up. Therefore, as we have opportunity, let us do good to all people, especially to those who belong to the family of believers."

Galatians 6:7-10 NIV

I have always found Paul's letter to the Galatians to be very practical, with advice that certainly can be applied to my own life. These verses are very plainly talking about how God wants us to treat others.....
"Do good to all people, especially to those who belong to the family of believers." ... I am so very grateful to be a part of that family! How about you?

Bonnie

July 17

"But because of his great love for us, God, who is rich in mercy, made us alive with Christ even when we were dead in transgressions—it is by grace you have been saved. And God raised us up with Christ and seated us with him in the heavenly realms in Christ Jesus, in order that in the coming ages he might show the incomparable riches of his grace, expressed in his kindness to us in Christ Jesus. For it is by grace you have been saved, through faith—and this is not from yourselves, it is the gift of God— not by works, so that no one can boast. For we are God's handiwork, created in Christ Jesus to do good works, which God prepared in advance for us to do."

Ephesians 2:4-10 NIV

— ❖•❖ —

Beautiful reminder that everything good and praiseworthy in our lives, is not by our own power or ability, but rather by the Grace and Blessings from our Loving God! Keep this in mind as you pray for guidance in what He would lead YOU to do each day *Bonnie*

July 18

"Therefore, as God's chosen people, holy and dearly loved, clothe yourselves with compassion, kindness, humility, gentleness and patience. Bear with each other and forgive one another if any of you has a grievance against someone. Forgive as the Lord forgave you. And over all these virtues put on love, which binds them all together in perfect unity. Let the peace of Christ rule in your hearts, since as members of one body you were called to peace. And be thankful. Let the message of Christ dwell among you richly as you teach and admonish one another with all wisdom through psalms, hymns, and songs from the Spirit, singing to God with gratitude in your hearts. And whatever you do, whether in word or deed, do it all in the name of the Lord Jesus, giving thanks to God the Father through him."

Colossians 3:12-17 NIV

Giving Thanks today for Christ my Savior! No other precious blessings compare to His Love and Salvation!!

Bonnie

213.

July 19

"May the God of hope fill you with all joy and peace as you trust in him, so that you may overflow with hope by the power of the Holy Spirit."

Romans 15:13 NIV

No matter what you are facing today, our Lord can provide genuine joy and peace! My prayer is that we would always "trust in Him!"

Bonnie

July 20

"Rejoice in the Lord always. I will say it again: Rejoice! Let your gentleness be evident to all. The Lord is near. Do not be anxious about anything, but in every situation, by prayer and petition, with thanksgiving, present your requests to God. And the peace of God, which transcends all understanding, will guard your hearts and your minds in Christ Jesus. Finally, brothers and sisters, whatever is true, whatever is noble, whatever is right, whatever is pure, whatever is lovely, whatever is admirable—if anything is excellent or praiseworthy—think about such things."

Philippians 4:4-8 NIV

Today I am sharing these verses because I MYSELF NEED this reminder! Wow! I can get so wrapped up with details about STUFF!! When PEOPLE are what really MATTER!!! I certainly need to clean up my house better than it is, but MUCH MORE URGENT is the cleansing of my heart and mind!! I must allow HIM to truly "guard my heart and mind." So, I am DETERMINED to swing the doors of my heart and mind Wide Open, so JESUS has free access... ALWAYS!! *Bonnie*

July 21

"Be patient, then, brothers and sisters, until the Lord's coming. See how the farmer waits for the land to yield its valuable crop, patiently waiting for the autumn and spring rains. You too, be patient and stand firm, because the Lord's coming is near. Don't grumble against one another, brothers and sisters, or you will be judged. The Judge is standing at the door!"

James 5:7-9 NIV

The Epistle of James is packed with wisdom like this, in all 5 chapters. As we go on our long—awaited family vacation, I plan to read and study the book of James for my personal study. As I focus on family time, I will NOT be sending out daily messages until next week. So I am inviting YOU TO ALSO read and study James. So, till next week... "be patient and stand firm!" God Bless You! Love and Prayers,

Bonnie

July 22

"Out of the depths I cry to you, Lord; Lord, hear my voice. Let your ears be attentive to my cry for mercy. If you, Lord, kept a record of sins, Lord, who could stand? But with you there is forgiveness, so that we can, with reverence, serve you. I wait for the Lord, my whole being waits, and in his word I put my hope. I wait for the Lord more than watchmen wait for the morning, more than watchmen wait for the morning. Israel, put your hope in the Lord, for with the Lord is unfailing love and with him is full redemption. He himself will redeem Israel from all their sins."

Psalms 130:1-8 NIV

Reading thru some Psalms this morning, and I just felt that someone needs to hear these Words today. Our Merciful God hears us when we call on Him for help!

Bonnie

July 23

"Therefore, since we are surrounded by such a great cloud of witnesses, let us throw off everything that hinders and the sin that so easily entangles. And let us run with perseverance the race marked out for us, fixing our eyes on Jesus, the pioneer and perfecter of faith. For the joy set before him he endured the cross, scorning its shame, and sat down at the right hand of the throne of God. Consider him who endured such opposition from sinners, so that you will not grow weary and lose heart."

Hebrews 12:1-3 NIV

This morning I started a devotional that is written by Olympics athletes and picks up specifically on this Scripture passage. The athlete interviewed today emphasized treating our bodies as the Temple of God (which is of course a very scriptural metaphor.)

Bonnie

July 24

"May the God of hope fill you with all joy and peace as you trust in him, so that you may overflow with hope by the power of the Holy Spirit."

Romans 15:13 NIV

Some days it seems so easy to get discouraged about the smallest details that simply did not go our way, or things are not happening when and how we want them to. It is then we need to pause and remember that we worship and serve "The God of Hope!" The Hope that He offers will last for eternity!!

Bonnie

July 25

"May the God of hope fill you with all joy and peace as you trust in him, so that you may overflow with hope by the power of the Holy Spirit."

Romans 15:13 NIV

Some days it seems so easy to get discouraged about the smallest details that simply did not go our way, or things are not happening when and how we want them to. It is then we need to pause and remember that we worship and serve "The God of Hope!" The Hope that He offers will last for eternity!!

220.

Bonnie

Bonnie's Chocolate Chip Cookie Secret

I get asked this often and I honestly use the recipe on the back of the Nestle's semisweet Chocolate Chip bag!!! (I don't do exact measurements for the flour or chocolate chips··· I just keep adding the flour till I think the dough "feels right" to me ··· about the consistency of soft play doh. and I just add Chocolate Chips as liberally as I feel like doing it that day. Remember to add the LOVE··· by thinking of the ones who will be eating the cookies! Shape into balls and bake at 375 degrees just like package says. I take them out at 10 minutes and Let Them Cool On The Cookie Sheet! Then remove to paper towels to finish cooling. Store in ziplock bags in refrigerator (if there are any left that day!

Bonnie

"For God so loved the world that he gave his one and only Son, that whoever believes in him shall not perish but have eternal life. For God did not send his Son into the world to condemn the world, but to save the world through him. Whoever believes in him is not condemned, but whoever does not believe stands condemned already because they have not believed in the name of God's one and only Son. This is the verdict: Light has come into the world, but people loved darkness instead of light because their deeds were evil. Everyone who does evil hates the light, and will not come into the light for fear that their deeds will be exposed. But whoever lives by the truth comes into the light, so that it may be seen plainly that what they have done has been done in the sight of God."

John 3:16-21 NIV

Back to the basics of the Gospel··· John 3:16 is the first verse I remember memorizing.

Bonnie

July 27

"Let love and faithfulness never leave you; bind them around your neck, write them on the tablet of your heart. Then you will win favor and a good name in the sight of God and man. Trust in the Lord with all your heart and lean not on your own understanding; in all your ways submit to him, and he will make your paths straight."

Proverbs 3:3-6 NIV

This is a good message for our young people··· but also for adults at ANY age!!

223.

Bonnie

July 27

"Yes, my soul, find rest in God; my hope comes from him. Truly he is my rock and my salvation; he is my fortress, I will not be shaken. My salvation and my honor depend on God; he is my mighty rock, my refuge. Trust in him at all times, you people; pour out your hearts to him, for God is our refuge."

Psalms 62:5-8 NIV

Surely I am not the only one who needs to be reminded of this today!

Bonnie

July 28

"Finally, be strong in the Lord and in his mighty power. Put on the full armor of God, so that you can take your stand against the devil's schemes. For our struggle is not against flesh and blood, but against the rulers, against the authorities, against the powers of this dark world and against the spiritual forces of evil in the heavenly realms. Therefore put on the full armor of God, so that when the day of evil comes, you may be able to stand your ground, and after you have done everything, to stand. Stand firm then, with the belt of truth buckled around your waist, with the breastplate of righteousness in place, and with your feet fitted with the readiness that comes from the gospel of peace. In addition to all this, take up the shield of faith, with which you can extinguish all the flaming arrows of the evil one. Take the helmet of salvation and the sword of the Spirit, which is the word of God."

Ephesians 6:10-17 NIV

This is a great challenge as we face a new week! I appreciate "word pictures" ···illustrations like this that challenge us to live out our faith in our everyday lives! At the end of this day, what will you be able to talk to God about, that YOU have done with this day He has given you? It's a question I will have to ask myself also!

Bonnie

225.

July 28

"Come, let us sing for joy to the Lord; let us shout aloud to the Rock of our salvation. Let us come before him with thanksgiving and extol him with music and song. For the Lord is the great God, the great King above all gods. In his hand are the depths of the earth, and the mountain peaks belong to him. The sea is his, for he made it, and his hands formed the dry land. Come, let us bow down in worship, let us kneel before the Lord our Maker; for he is our God and we are the people of his pasture, the flock under his care...."

Psalms 95:1-7 NIV

—◆·◆—

Have a great day, thanking Our Creator for all His wonders and blessings!

Bonnie

226.

July 29

"One of the teachers of the law came and heard them debating. Noticing that Jesus had given them a good answer, he asked him, "Of all the commandments, which is the most important?" "The most important one," answered Jesus, "is this: 'Hear, O Israel: The Lord our God, the Lord is one. Love the Lord your God with all your heart and with all your soul and with all your mind and with all your strength.' The second is this: 'Love your neighbor as yourself.' There is no commandment greater than these.""

Mark 12:28-31 NIV

Today is my Bud's 75th Birthday! ('21) And I chose these verses today because I have witnessed that this is how Bud strives to live his life! And I am so very blessed to walk along beside him!

Bonnie

This man right here ⋯ this farmer⋯ this Christian man with a big caring heart⋯ My Bud⋯ is 75 today! Happy Birthday to the man I love!!

July 30

"Be patient, then, brothers and sisters, until the Lord's coming. See how the farmer waits for the land to yield its valuable crop, patiently waiting for the autumn and spring rains. You too, be patient and stand firm, because the Lord's coming is near. Don't grumble against one another, brothers and sisters, or you will be judged. The Judge is standing at the door!"

James 5:7-9 NIV

We arrived home Friday evening from a wonderful family vacation; it was Bud's birthday, and in the midst of unpacking and starting laundry, we went for a long pleasant drive... as "the farmer" viewed his crops, we talked about our many blessings... among them, the growing corn, beans, children and grandchildren... plus great-grandchildren!! Feeling very blessed and grateful! I hope that you appreciated the Words of Wisdom and encouragement from reading from the Epistle of James each day this past week, as I did. ... Have a great day of worship Sunday, and I will plan to reconnect with you on Monday. Meanwhile, "Stand firm, because the Lord's coming is near!"

Bonnie

July 31

"Then Jesus came to them and said, "All authority in heaven and on earth has been given to me. Therefore go and make disciples of all nations, baptizing them in the name of the Father and of the Son and of the Holy Spirit, and teaching them to obey everything I have commanded you. And surely I am with you always, to the very end of the age.""

Matthew 28:18-20 NIV.

It is good to be reminded that to some extent each Christian is a missionary!

Bonnie

This pic is crazy, with my white hair blending with the water spraying in back of boat! Fun times!

Bonnie

August

August 1

""Be silent before me, you islands! Let the nations renew their strength! Let them come forward and speak; let us meet together at the place of judgment. "Who has stirred up one from the east, calling him in righteousness to his service? He hands nations over to him and subdues kings before him. He turns them to dust with his sword, to windblown chaff with his bow. He pursues them and moves on unscathed, by a path his feet have not traveled before. Who has done this and carried it through, calling forth the generations from the beginning? I, the Lord—with the first of them and with the last—I am he.""

Isaiah 41:1-4 NIV.

With all the travel and interaction that naturally occurs during the Olympics, there are valuable opportunities for God's people to share The Gospel.

Bonnie

August 2

"Blessed is the one who does not walk in step with the wicked or stand in the way that sinners take or sit in the company of mockers, but whose delight is in the law of the Lord, and who meditates on his law day and night. That person is like a tree planted by streams of water, which yields its fruit in season and whose leaf does not wither—whatever they do prospers. Not so the wicked! They are like chaff that the wind blows away. Therefore the wicked will not stand in the judgment, nor sinners in the assembly of the righteous. For the Lord watches over the way of the righteous, but the way of the wicked leads to destruction."

Psalms 1:1-6 NIV

Indeed we each have a choice... and I choose to delight in The Lord, and His Ways... How about you?!?

Bonnie

August 3

"For the grace of God has appeared that offers salvation to all people. It teaches us to say "No" to ungodliness and worldly passions, and to live self-controlled, upright and godly lives in this present age, while we wait for the blessed hope—the appearing of the glory of our great God and Savior, Jesus Christ, who gave himself for us to redeem us from all wickedness and to purify for himself a people that are his very own, eager to do what is good. These, then, are the things you should teach. Encourage and rebuke with all authority. Do not let anyone despise you."

Titus 2:11-15 NIV

These are verses that I don't read often, but the advice is worth sharing; we all need to be "eager to do what is good!"

Bonnie

233.

August 4

"Now all has been heard; here is the conclusion of the matter:
Fear God and keep his commandments, for this is the duty of all
mankind. For God will bring every deed into judgment, including
every hidden thing, whether it is good or evil."

Ecclesiastes 12:13-14 NIV

Whenever I read this, I am reminded that My Lord knows even all my
thoughts! This means even though what I say and do openly might be
(or seem) honorable, God knows even my secret thoughts and desires.
So my earnest prayer is, "Lord, Please take control of it all! Help me in
my weakness, and guide me in my actions and speech!" *Bonnie*

234.

Bonnie's Blessings

August 5

"So do not throw away your confidence; it will be richly rewarded. You need to persevere so that when you have done the will of God, you will receive what he has promised. For, "In just a little while, he who is coming will come and will not delay." And, "But my righteous one will live by faith. And I take no pleasure in the one who shrinks back." But we do not belong to those who shrink back and are destroyed, but to those who have faith and are saved."

Hebrews 10:35-39 NIV

This passage was written to early Christians who has faced the threat of severe persecution, but were bravely true to the Living God. I want to display that kind of CONFIDENCE in The Living God. I keep remembering the words of an old hymn that said: "Cast not away your confidence, says The Lord Our God!"

Bonnie

August 6

"Submit to one another out of reverence for Christ. Wives, submit yourselves to your own husbands as you do to the Lord. For the husband is the head of the wife as Christ is the head of the church, his body, of which he is the Savior. Now as the church submits to Christ, so also wives should submit to their husbands in everything. Husbands, love your wives, just as Christ loved the church and gave himself up for her to make her holy, cleansing her by the washing with water through the word, and to present her to himself as a radiant church, without stain or wrinkle or any other blemish, but holy and blameless. In this same way, husbands ought to love their wives as their own bodies. He who loves his wife loves himself."

Ephesians 5:21:28 NIV

On this date 55 years ago, ('22) Bud and I said "I DO" in our home church in Lincoln. It is a "profound mystery"... and I am so blessed to share it with him! Yet even MORE "profound" is the love we are able to share for Christ and His Church! It's a good life, despite every bump or curve along the way. Thank You, Lord!

Bonnie

236.

August 7

"Let the peace of Christ rule in your hearts, since as members of one body you were called to peace. And be thankful. Let the message of Christ dwell among you richly as you teach and admonish one another with all wisdom through psalms, hymns, and songs from the Spirit, singing to God with gratitude in your hearts. And whatever you do, whether in word or deed, do it all in the name of the Lord Jesus, giving thanks to God the Father through him."

Colossians 3:15-17 NIV

This year, I keep returning to this chapter··· finding this letter to these early Christians still so applicable to my life today··· and yours! Praising Him with gratitude in my heart! How about you? Praying you feel blessed today also.   237.   *Bonnie*

August 8

"I know what it is to be in need, and I know what it is to have plenty. I have learned the secret of being content in any and every situation, whether well fed or hungry, whether living in plenty or in want. I can do all this through him who gives me strength."

Philippians 4:12-13 NIV

We can learn so much from these verses about "being content" in every circumstance. Our God is able to give us the strength we need.... No Matter What!! I am leaning on this truth today... how about you?

Bonnie

Bonnie's Blessings

"You were taught, with regard to your former way of life, to put off your old self, which is being corrupted by its deceitful desires; to be made new in the attitude of your minds; and to put on the new self, created to be like God in true righteousness and holiness. Therefore each of you must put off falsehood and speak truthfully to your neighbor, for we are all members of one body. "In your anger do not sin": Do not let the sun go down while you are still angry, and do not give the devil a foothold. Anyone who has been stealing must steal no longer, but must work, doing something useful with their own hands, that they may have something to share with those in need. Do not let any unwholesome talk come out of your mouths, but only what is helpful for building others up according to their needs, that it may benefit those who listen. And do not grieve the Holy Spirit of God, with whom you were sealed for the day of redemption. Get rid of all bitterness, rage and anger, brawling and slander, along with every form of malice. Be kind and compassionate to one another, forgiving each other, just as in Christ God forgave you."

Ephesians 4:22-32 NIV

While reading this, I find it so easy to think "well, I don't do this or that!" But with that attitude, I entirely miss the point that every single one of us has room to grow, in order to be more like Christ··· the One Who gave His own life in order that we might be saved from our own unrighteousness! Let's each praise Him for that, and be submissive··· searching our own hearts, and leaning on Him to help us grow to be more like Jesus every day!!

Bonnie

239.

August 10

"For this reason I kneel before the Father, from whom every family in heaven and on earth derives its name. I pray that out of his glorious riches he may strengthen you with power through his Spirit in your inner being, so that Christ may dwell in your hearts through faith. And I pray that you, being rooted and established in love, may have power, together with all the Lord's holy people, to grasp how wide and long and high and deep is the love of Christ, and to know this love that surpasses knowledge—that you may be filled to the measure of all the fullness of God. Now to him who is able to do immeasurably more than all we ask or imagine, according to his power that is at work within us, to him be glory in the church and in Christ Jesus throughout all generations, for ever and ever! Amen."

Ephesians 3:14-21 NIV

The Apostle Paul penned the words of this beautiful prayer··· we can also pray this for each other!··· A phrase in the midst of this prayer reminds me of a chorus I learned at church camp years ago:

"Deep and Wide, Deep and Wide! There's a Fountain flowing Deep and Wide!"

240.

Bonnie

August 11

""This, then, is how you should pray: " 'Our Father in heaven, hallowed be your name, your kingdom come, your will be done, on earth as it is in heaven. Give us today our daily bread. And forgive us our debts, as we also have forgiven our debtors. And lead us not into temptation, but deliver us from the evil one. ' For if you forgive other people when they sin against you, your heavenly Father will also forgive you. But if you do not forgive others their sins, your Father will not forgive your sins."

Matthew 6:9-15 NIV

───────◆·◆───────

Thank You, Almighty God, that You have made a way for us to approach Your Throne through prayer, knowing that YOU Are Able to hear us and to meet our every need, and much more besides! Amen

Bonnie

August 12

"You have searched me, Lord, and you know me. You know when I sit and when I rise; you perceive my thoughts from afar. You discern my going out and my lying down; you are familiar with all my ways. Before a word is on my tongue you, Lord, know it completely. You hem me in behind and before, and you lay your hand upon me.

Psalms 139:1-5 NIV

For you created my inmost being; you knit me together in my mother's womb. I praise you because I am fearfully and wonderfully made; your works are wonderful, I know that full well. My frame was not hidden from you when I was made in the secret place, when I was woven together in the depths of the earth. Your eyes saw my unformed body; all the days ordained for me were written in your book before one of them came to be.

Psalms 139:13-16 NIV

Thank You, Almighty God, that You have made a way for us to approach Your Throne through prayer, knowing that YOU Are Able to hear us and to meet our every need, and much more besides! Amen

Bonnie

August 13

"We wait in hope for the Lord; he is our help and our shield. In him our hearts rejoice, for we trust in his holy name. May your unfailing love be with us, Lord, even as we put our hope in you."

Psalms 33:20-22 NIV

—◆·◆—

Praying your day is filled with such Love and Hope!

Bonnie

August 14

"Rejoice in the Lord always. I will say it again: Rejoice! Let your gentleness be evident to all. The Lord is near. Do not be anxious about anything, but in every situation, by prayer and petition, with thanksgiving, present your requests to God. And the peace of God, which transcends all understanding, will guard your hearts and your minds in Christ Jesus."

Philippians 4:4-7 NIV

— ◆·◆ —

Lord, I pray that this will be my mindset today, as we go to see the specialist at SLU concerning my memory issues. In all things, Lord, let us give You all the glory!

Bonnie

August 15

"Remind the people to be subject to rulers and authorities, to be obedient, to be ready to do whatever is good, to slander no one, to be peaceable and considerate, and always to be gentle toward everyone. At one time we too were foolish, disobedient, deceived and enslaved by all kinds of passions and pleasures. We lived in malice and envy, being hated and hating one another. But when the kindness and love of God our Savior appeared, he saved us, not because of righteous things we had done, but because of his mercy. He saved us through the washing of rebirth and renewal by the Holy Spirit, whom he poured out on us generously through Jesus Christ our Savior, so that, having been justified by his grace, we might become heirs having the hope of eternal life. This is a trustworthy saying. And I want you to stress these things, so that those who have trusted in God may be careful to devote themselves to doing what is good. These things are excellent and profitable for everyone."

Titus 3:1-8 NIV

Such practical instructions on how we should live our lives! Also, this letter that the Apostle Paul wrote to Titus is only 3 chapters long, so you can easily read it in one sitting... I did just now! *Bonnie*

245.

August 15

"Therefore, since we have been justified through faith, we have peace with God through our Lord Jesus Christ, through whom we have gained access by faith into this grace in which we now stand. And we boast in the hope of the glory of God. Not only so, but we also glory in our sufferings, because we know that suffering produces perseverance; perseverance, character; and character, hope. And hope does not put us to shame, because God's love has been poured out into our hearts through the Holy Spirit, who has been given to us."

Romans 5:1-5 NIV

These verses are powerful and encouraging! Right now, in my mid 70s, I no longer can memorize Scripture well, but I am going to focus on memorizing these verses about hope and peace and perseverance.

Bonnie

246.

August 16

"I lift up my eyes to the mountains— where does my help come from? My help comes from the Lord, the Maker of heaven and earth. He will not let your foot slip— he who watches over you will not slumber; indeed, he who watches over Israel will neither slumber nor sleep. The Lord watches over you— the Lord is your shade at your right hand; the sun will not harm you by day, nor the moon by night. The Lord will keep you from all harm— he will watch over your life; the Lord will watch over your coming and going both now and forevermore."

Psalms 121:1-8 NIV

A very dear friend and prayer warrior sent this Psalm to me early this morning, and I just wanted to pass this blessing on to the rest of you. The Lord will "watch over your life" also! THANK YOU Jesus! Amen.

247.

Bonnie

August 17

"Children are a gift from The Lord; they are a reward from Him."
Psalm 127:3 NIV

This verse was never more real to me than on this day years ago when our firstborn arrived and we finally held our Wendy Charlene in our arms!!! She continues to be a blessing to so many, in very special ways with all her God-given talents! Feeling very blessed by many Precious memories! God is so good!

Birthday Blessings to the beautiful brown eyed girl who made me a Mommy. We LOVE our Wendy!

Bonnie

August 18

"People were bringing little children to Jesus for him to place his hands on them, but the disciples rebuked them. When Jesus saw this, he was indignant. He said to them, "Let the little children come to me, and do not hinder them, for the kingdom of God belongs to such as these. Truly I tell you, anyone who will not receive the kingdom of God like a little child will never enter it." And he took the children in his arms, placed his hands on them and blessed them."

Mark 10:13-16 NIV

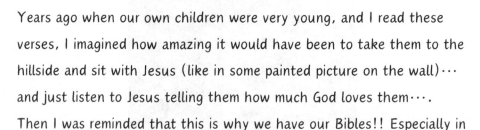

Years ago when our own children were very young, and I read these verses, I imagined how amazing it would have been to take them to the hillside and sit with Jesus (like in some painted picture on the wall)···
and just listen to Jesus telling them how much God loves them····.
Then I was reminded that this is why we have our Bibles!! Especially in America··· for now at least··· we have the freedom to share The Gospel··· not only with innocent children, but also with adults in need.
Meanwhile we hear of those in some parts of the world who literally risk their lives to do so!! We all need to treasure and share The Word!
And pray for those who are persecuted for doing the same!!

Bonnie

August 19

"The Lord is compassionate and gracious, slow to anger, abounding in love. He will not always accuse, nor will he harbor his anger forever; he does not treat us as our sins deserve or repay us according to our iniquities. For as high as the heavens are above the earth, so great is his love for those who fear him; as far as the east is from the west, so far has he removed our transgressions from us. As a father has compassion on his children, so the Lord has compassion on those who fear him; for he knows how we are formed, he remembers that we are dust. The life of mortals is like grass, they flourish like a flower of the field; the wind blows over it and it is gone, and its place remembers it no more. But from everlasting to everlasting the Lord's love is with those who fear him, and his righteousness with their children's children— with those who keep his covenant and remember to obey his precepts."

Psalms 103:8-18 NIV

———— ◆•◆ ————

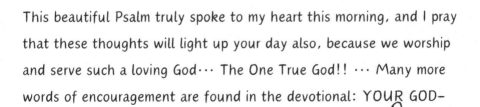

This beautiful Psalm truly spoke to my heart this morning, and I pray that these thoughts will light up your day also, because we worship and serve such a loving God··· The One True God!! ··· Many more words of encouragement are found in the devotional: YOUR GOD-GIVEN VALUE by C Rechele LaD

Bonnie

250.

August 20

"And you, _____, also were included in Christ when you heard the message of truth, the gospel of your salvation. When you believed, you were marked in him with a seal, the promised Holy Spirit, who is a deposit guaranteeing our inheritance until the redemption of those who are God's possession—to the praise of his glory."

Ephesians 1:13-14 NIV

One devotion that I read this morning suggested that you read these verses aloud—– and Insert Your Own Name in the blank space added here. I did so, and it was quite powerful, and humbling! ····. Thank You, Lord for Your sacrifice!!

251.

Bonnie

August 21

"The Lord himself goes before you and will be with you; he will never leave you nor forsake you. Do not be afraid; do not be discouraged.""

Deuteronomy 31:8 NIV

These were powerful words spoken to the Israelites as they were about to go into battle, even facing giants! Some days, our problems may seem to loom before us like giants!!! But we serve this same God!! And He Is ABLE!! He Is MIGHTY! He Is EVERLASTING!!! So, do not be afraid and do not be discouraged! Praise God for all the Good HE has poured into your life, and march on through the day!! Our God Walks Beside You!!

252.

Bonnie

August 22

"The Lord makes firm the steps of the one who delights in him; though he may stumble, he will not fall, for the Lord upholds him with his hand. I was young and now I am old, yet I have never seen the righteous forsaken or their children begging bread. They are always generous and lend freely; their children will be a blessing."

Psalms 37:23-26 NIV

Like my dear mother Maxine, I have always loved the Psalms, and 37 is one of my favorites... So I quote from it today, to comment that our children are Definitely a Blessing!!

Bonnie

August 23

"My son, do not forget my teaching, but keep my commands in your heart, for they will prolong your life many years and bring you peace and prosperity. Let love and faithfulness never leave you; bind them around your neck, write them on the tablet of your heart. Then you will win favor and a good name in the sight of God and man. Trust in the Lord with all your heart and lean not on your own understanding; in all your ways submit to him, and he will make your paths straight. Do not be wise in your own eyes; fear the Lord and shun evil. This will bring health to your body and nourishment to your bones. Honor the Lord with your wealth, with the firstfruits of all your crops; then your barns will be filled to overflowing, and your vats will brim over with new wine.

Proverbs 3:1-10 NIV

As this new school year gets underway, let's all be in prayer for the teachers and students to be diligent as they "seek wisdom"; and meanwhile, I pray that each one of us would Truly TRUST THE LORD...and NOT lean on our own understanding!!! Please take time today to focus some of your prayers on the safety and peaceful atmosphere which we would all desire to have in All Our School Classrooms!!

Bonnie

August 24

""You are the salt of the earth. But if the salt loses its saltiness, how can it be made salty again? It is no longer good for anything, except to be thrown out and trampled underfoot. "You are the light of the world. A town built on a hill cannot be hidden. Neither do people light a lamp and put it under a bowl. Instead they put it on its stand, and it gives light to everyone in the house. In the same way, let your light shine before others, that they may see your good deeds and glorify your Father in heaven."

Matthew 5:13-16 NIV

＊・＊

These Words of Jesus are such great reminders of how we should live!
··· Also, this makes me smile, remembering the song learned as a child
(with actions!) "This Little Light of Mine! I'm Gonna Let It Shine!"

Bonnie

August 25

"There is a time for everything, and a season for every activity under the heavens: a time to be born and a time to die, a time to plant and a time to uproot, a time to kill and a time to heal, a time to tear down and a time to build, a time to weep and a time to laugh, a time to mourn and a time to dance, a time to scatter stones and a time to gather them, a time to embrace and a time to refrain from embracing, a time to search and a time to give up, a time to keep and a time to throw away, a time to tear and a time to mend, a time to be silent and a time to speak, a time to love and a time to hate, a time for war and a time for peace. What do workers gain from their toil? I have seen the burden God has laid on the human race. He has made everything beautiful in its time. He has also set eternity in the human heart; yet no one can fathom what God has done from beginning to end."

Ecclesiastes 3:1-11 NIV

These words are so profound, and even poetic; I even like to read them aloud. HOWEVER, I am grateful that God's Message is not completely wrapped up in this dynamic poetry...BECAUSE.... Then CHRIST CAME!!

Bonnie

August 26

"Consider it pure joy, my brothers and sisters, whenever you face trials of many kinds, because you know that the testing of your faith produces perseverance. Let perseverance finish its work so that you may be mature and complete, not lacking anything. If any of you lacks wisdom, you should ask God, who gives generously to all without finding fault, and it will be given to you. But when you ask, you must believe and not doubt, because the one who doubts is like a wave of the sea, blown and tossed by the wind."

James 1:2-6 NIV

Good way to start the week··· with reminders from the practical inspired writings of James··· my favorite epistle.] Have a great week! I am starting mine with more substitute teaching.

Bonnie

257.

August 27

"So do not fear, for I am with you; do not be dismayed, for I am your God. I will strengthen you and help you; I will uphold you with my righteous right hand."

Isaiah 41:10 NIV

Great Words of encouragement, No Matter What your situation may be!! Hold on to HIS HAND!!

Bonnie

August 28

"Unless the Lord had given me help, I would soon have dwelt in the silence of death. When I said, "My foot is slipping," your unfailing love, Lord, supported me. When anxiety was great within me, your consolation brought me joy."

Psalms 94:17-19 NIV

―――――― ◆·◆ ――――――

While my problems are small compared to many others, they are very real to me. Also, when I am accustomed to helping others――even having worked in a professional field doing so―― it is very difficult to relinquish decisions to others, and to realize my dependence on others, even some days to recall basic plans, or names, or directions, etc!! Some days are "foggier" than others. But EVERY DAY, my God and my Bud··· and our amazing children and grandchildren···are so patient and helpful; also we are getting professional help, as I have mentioned before.] MEANWHILE··· for our 55th Anniversary Bud had asked if I wanted jewelry or something else, and I requested a special getaway in Branson for just the two of us··· so that's where we will be, leaving early tomorrow. With My Love and Prayers,

Bonnie

August 29

"Why, my soul, are you downcast? Why so disturbed within me? Put your hope in God, for I will yet praise him, my Savior and my God."

Psalms 42:11 NIV.

— ✦·✦ —

No Matter What··· We have an amazing God Who loves and cares for us deeply!! Let us praise Him today.

Bonnie

August 30

"Brothers and sisters, I do not consider myself yet to have taken hold of it. But one thing I do: Forgetting what is behind and straining toward what is ahead, I press on toward the goal to win the prize for which God has called me heavenward in Christ Jesus."

Philippians 3:13-14 NIV

These special verses came to my mind after watching our USA Wheelchair Rugby team winning their first game as they Go for the Gold in Tokyo! Each team member was giving their best effort, and they were rewarded with a win! Even More So, we need to each one give our all in the "Game of Life" ··· pressing on towards the prize as we serve The Lord! Our eternal reward is even so much greater than the gold we expect Chuck Melton and his team partners to bring home from Tokyo!!

Bonnie

261.

August 31

""Blessed are the poor in spirit, for theirs is the kingdom of heaven. Blessed are those who mourn, for they will be comforted. Blessed are the meek, for they will inherit the earth. Blessed are those who hunger and thirst for righteousness, for they will be filled. Blessed are the merciful, for they will be shown mercy. Blessed are the pure in heart, for they will see God. Blessed are the peacemakers, for they will be called children of God. Blessed are those who are persecuted because of righteousness, for theirs is the kingdom of heaven. "Blessed are you when people insult you, persecute you and falsely say all kinds of evil against you because of me. Rejoice and be glad, because great is your reward in heaven, for in the same way they persecuted the prophets who were before you."

Matthew 5:3-12 NIV

Jesus proclaimed these truths long before the tragic persecution that we hear about in the news reports today··· but His Promises still ring true: "Great is your reward in Heaven."

Bonnie

262.

September

September 1

"The LORD is my light and my salvation; whom shall I fear?
The LORD is the strength of my life; of whom shall I be
afraid?"

Psalm 27:1 KJV

Whatever we are facing··· whether it is a specific hardship or fear of

the unknown···The Lord is with us··· So, of whom shall we be

afraid??! Praying you will trust Him to be your Guide through it all.

Bonnie

264.

September 2

"For if you remain silent at this time, relief and deliverance for the Jews will arise from another place, but you and your father's family will perish. And who knows but that you have come to your royal position for such a time as this?""

Esther 4:14 NIV.

Hello! Esther.... what an inspiration!!

Bud and I had a great getaway in Branson... came home a couple days early, and enjoyed some catching up and activities back here as well. Now getting back to a routine and looking forward to harvest time before long! Plus major happy wedding plans in our family! That's not to say we are without problems or illnesses or setbacks in the Klockenga Clan!!! Far from it!! But Our God Is Faithful, just as He was in the time of Esther and her people. HE NEVER LEAVES US! And I believe the HE has a plan for each of us... we need to be aware of the opportunities He places before us; we too can proclaim His Truth, and be ready to help others, in "such a time as this!"

With My Love and Prayers,

Bonnie

September 3

"Have mercy on me, my God, have mercy on me, for in you I take refuge. I will take refuge in the shadow of your wings until the disaster has passed. I cry out to God Most High, to God, who vindicates me. He sends from heaven and saves me, rebuking those who hotly pursue me— God sends forth his love and his faithfulness. I am in the midst of lions; I am forced to dwell among ravenous beasts— men whose teeth are spears and arrows, whose tongues are sharp swords. Be exalted, O God, above the heavens; let your glory be over all the earth. They spread a net for my feet— I was bowed down in distress. They dug a pit in my path— but they have fallen into it themselves. My heart, O God, is steadfast, my heart is steadfast; I will sing and make music. Awake, my soul! Awake, harp and lyre! I will awaken the dawn. I will praise you, Lord, among the nations; I will sing of you among the peoples. For great is your love, reaching to the heavens; your faithfulness reaches to the skies. Be exalted, O God, above the heavens; let your glory be over all the earth."

Psalms 57:1-11 NIV

The Words of this Psalm, it seems, can speak to the heart of ANYONE, in ANY SITUATION.... because we ALL have problems AND joys.... We ALL need His Mercy. And we EACH need to eagerly PRAISE HIM... in the midst of each trial AND each victory!! Let Us Praise The Lord Today, through All we Say and Do!! Amen

Bonnie

September 4

"Be patient, then, brothers and sisters, until the Lord's coming. See how the farmer waits for the land to yield its valuable crop, patiently waiting for the autumn and spring rains. You too, be patient and stand firm, because the Lord's coming is near. Don't grumble against one another, brothers and sisters, or you will be judged. The Judge is standing at the door!"

James 5:7-9 NIV

Each morning for my time of Bible reading and devotions, my favorite spot is on our comfy couch, looking out the tall glass front door ····. My view includes a tall tree in the yard, and a large field just across the road. This year Bud has planted soybeans in that field; next year it will probably be corn. This morning I see the leaves that are starting to change colors, from bright green to yellow, as they mature. I also like to go for rides with my farmer, as he surveys the other fields to check on their progress, "waiting for the land to yield its valuable crop." And as I read verses like these today, I am reminded that Our Lord is even much more carefully observing our growth and progress towards maturity. Our God desires for us to flourish and grow and multiply. We need to be alert and responding to His care and His plans. Meanwhile, He also calls for more workers in His fields! There is sooo much work still to be done! Lord, help us to "be patient and stand firm, because the Lord's coming is near!!"

Bonnie

September 5

"But if we walk in the light, as he is in the light, we have fellowship with one another, and the blood of Jesus, his Son, purifies us from all sin. If we claim to be without sin, we deceive ourselves and the truth is not in us."

1 John 1:7-8 NIV

A devotion I read recently refers to these verses, and other passages, to remind us that we need to be open with each other, acknowledging that none of us are without sin. We all need Christ as our Savior... and it helps us in our daily lives to also have friends with whom we can be transparent! Let your Light Shine for Jesus today! And enjoy the fellowship!

Bonnie

268.

September 6

"So then, just as you received Christ Jesus as Lord, continue to live your lives in him, rooted and built up in him, strengthened in the faith as you were taught, and overflowing with thankfulness. See to it that no one takes you captive through hollow and deceptive philosophy, which depends on human tradition and the elemental spiritual forces of this world rather than on Christ. For in Christ all the fullness of the Deity lives in bodily form, and in Christ you have been brought to fullness. He is the head over every power and authority."

Colossians 2:6-10 NIV

With all the negative forces at work in the world today, this letter could have been written directly to us! We need to be alert to all the evil surrounding us, and be rooted deeply in His Word!

Bonnie

269.

September 7

"As the deer pants for streams of water, so my soul pants for you, my God. My soul thirsts for God, for the living God. When can I go and meet with God? My tears have been my food day and night, while people say to me all day long, "Where is your God?" These things I remember as I pour out my soul: how I used to go to the house of God under the protection of the Mighty One with shouts of joy and praise among the festive throng. Why, my soul, are you downcast? Why so disturbed within me? Put your hope in God, for I will yet praise him, my Savior and my God. My soul is downcast within me; therefore I will remember you from the land of the Jordan, the heights of Hermon—from Mount Mizar. Deep calls to deep in the roar of your waterfalls; all your waves and breakers have swept over me. By day the Lord directs his love, at night his song is with me— a prayer to the God of my life. I say to God my Rock, "Why have you forgotten me? Why must I go about mourning, oppressed by the enemy?" My bones suffer mortal agony as my foes taunt me, saying to me all day long, "Where is your God?" Why, my soul, are you downcast? Why so disturbed within me? Put your hope in God, for I will yet praise him, my Savior and my God."

Psalms 42:1-11 NIV

Somehow, each time I read this precious Psalm, it refreshes me anew! Praying that these Words soothe your soul as well...and Put Your Hope In God!   270.   *Bonnie*

September 8

"Then the eleven disciples went to Galilee, to the mountain where Jesus had told them to go. When they saw him, they worshiped him; but some doubted. Then Jesus came to them and said, "All authority in heaven and on earth has been given to me. Therefore go and make disciples of all nations, baptizing them in the name of the Father and of the Son and of the Holy Spirit, and teaching them to obey everything I have commanded you. And surely I am with you always, to the very end of the age.""

Matthew 28:16-20 NIV

Whenever I read these familiar Words, I love to imagine the thrill and majesty of being there in person! And I hope with all my heart that I would have left that mountain, immediately and eagerly spreading the Good News about Jesus Our Savior!!··· And then I remember that YES··· the mission continues! Till He calls me Home, THIS needs to be my focus!! Praise God!! HIS WORD IS TRUTH!!

Bonnie

September 9

"See to it, brothers and sisters, that none of you has a sinful, unbelieving heart that turns away from the living God. But encourage one another daily, as long as it is called "Today," so that none of you may be hardened by sin's deceitfulness. We have come to share in Christ, if indeed we hold our original conviction firmly to the very end."

Hebrews 3:12-14 NIV

We need to let our lives be a testimony of God's saving power, and encourage others to do the same. Personally, I could not have joy or peace in my heart without the saving grace of my Lord and Savior, Jesus Christ!

Bonnie

272.

September 10

"Wives, submit yourselves to your own husbands as you do to the Lord. For the husband is the head of the wife as Christ is the head of the church, his body, of which he is the Savior. Now as the church submits to Christ, so also wives should submit to their husbands in everything. Husbands, love your wives, just as Christ loved the church and gave himself up for her to make her holy, cleansing her by the washing with water through the word, and to present her to himself as a radiant church, without stain or wrinkle or any other blemish, but holy and blameless. In this same way, husbands ought to love their wives as their own bodies. He who loves his wife loves himself. After all, no one ever hated their own body, but they feed and care for their body, just as Christ does the church— for we are members of his body. "For this reason a man will leave his father and mother and be united to his wife, and the two will become one flesh." This is a profound mystery—but I am talking about Christ and the church. However, each one of you also must love his wife as he loves himself, and the wife must respect her husband."

Ephesians 5:22-33 NIV

Today I am sharing this beautiful passage, while our own family is naturally focused on a very special Wedding Day that is fast approaching. Still, this beautiful analogy can be a daily reminder of how much Christ loves us, to the point of "giving himself up for us!" Let's Praise HIM for such magnificent LOVE! And eagerly Trust and Obey and Serve Our Lord Jesus Christ!!

Bonnie

September 11

"I can do all things through Christ who gives me strength."

Philippians 4:13. NIV

Today (9/11), I am sharing a favorite verse from a friend who said this passage of Scripture helped to get thru her struggles when she was a single mom. My reason for posting it today, is that we all need that same strength as we walk through this day of unprecedented heartbreaking memories of the events of 9/11!!!

274.

Bonnie

September 12

Today being Sunday, I am posting a verse that a special Children's Minister lists as her "Life Verse" ⋯ (do you have a life verse)?⋯ This is so appropriate to share on Sunday morning:

"Let your light shine before men, that they may see your good works, and glorify your Father which is in Heaven."

Matthew 5:16 NIV

So I am praying that each of you have a great beginning of you week⋯ shining for Him. ⋯ Makes me want to hold up my imaginary candle and sing⋯ "This Little Light of mine, I'm gonna let it shine!"

Bonnie

September 13

"Likewise you younger people, submit yourselves to your elders. Yes, all of you be submissive to one another, and be clothed with humility, for "God resists the proud, But gives grace to the humble." Therefore humble yourselves under the mighty hand of God, that He may exalt you in due time, casting all your care upon Him, for He cares for you. Be sober, be vigilant; because your adversary the devil walks about like a roaring lion, seeking whom he may devour. Resist him, steadfast in the faith, knowing that the same sufferings are experienced by your brotherhood in the world. But may the God of all grace, who called us to His eternal glory by Christ Jesus, after you have suffered a while, perfect, establish, strengthen, and settle you. To Him be the glory and the dominion forever and ever. Amen."

I Peter 5:5-11 NKJV.

— ✦•✦ —

I LOVE THIS PART: "Cast all your cares on Him, for He Cares!"
(Our human friends may have good intentions··· but Jesus Cares about you and me!

Bonnie

September 14

"For all have sinned,and come short of the glory of God;
Being justified freely by his grace through the redemption
that is in Christ Jesus : Whom God hath set forth to be a
propitiation through Faith in his Blood, to declare his
righteousness for the remission of sins that are past,
through the forbearance of God.

Romans 3 : 23-25

Our Monday was very long but productive: Bud's pre-planned
surgery to replace his worn-out Pacemaker went very smoothly.
Praise God!] Now...Returning today to sharing favorite Bible
verses... one dear friend who has been thru much hardship shared
this scripture.

Bonnie

September 15

"For no matter how many promises God has made, they are "Yes" in Christ. And so through him the "Amen" is spoken by us to the glory of God. Now it is God who makes both us and you stand firm in Christ. He anointed us, set his seal of ownership on us, and put his Spirit in our hearts as a deposit, guaranteeing what is to come."

2 Corinthians 1:20-22 NIV

This very reassuring message was shared with me by one of the elders in our congregation at GCC····. I especially like the phrase "stand firm in Christ."

278.

Bonnie

September 16

"As for you, you were dead in your transgressions and sins, in which you used to live when you followed the ways of this world and of the ruler of the kingdom of the air, the spirit who is now at work in those who are disobedient. All of us also lived among them at one time, gratifying the cravings of our flesh and following its desires and thoughts. Like the rest, we were by nature deserving of wrath. But because of his great love for us, God, who is rich in mercy, made us alive with Christ even when we were dead in transgressions—it is by grace you have been saved. And God raised us up with Christ and seated us with him in the heavenly realms in Christ Jesus, in order that in the coming ages he might show the incomparable riches of his grace, expressed in his kindness to us in Christ Jesus. For it is by grace you have been saved, through faith—and this is not from yourselves, it is the gift of God— not by works, so that no one can boast. For we are God's handiwork, created in Christ Jesus to do good works, which God prepared in advance for us to do."

Ephesians 2:1-10 NIV

Focusing on the positive, as we start off a new week.... reminding ourselves that God made each one of us, and He has a purpose for our lives! There can be hope and satisfaction in each day, when we focus of praising and serving the One True God!! Everything else eventually falls into place when our ultimate goal is to worship and serve HIM!! Thank You, Jesus!!

279.

Bonnie

September 17

"God is our refuge and strength, an ever-present help in trouble. Therefore we will not fear."

Psalms 46:1-2a NIV

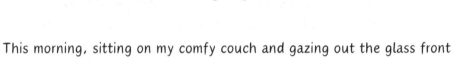

This morning, sitting on my comfy couch and gazing out the glass front door, I am watching a fog rapidly rolling In across the bean field, and it has almost totally blocked off my view, till all I can see is the tall oak tree a few yards from our front door. At the same time, my mind is very foggy this morning.... while I totally appreciate reading this favorite Psalm, I am struggling to remember what year it is! I check my datebook regularly to verify the month, day, and year. I know that I have another appointment today... in St Louis they will do an MRI... and I have had one before, so I am well aware that the procedure is simple and painless; I just need to lay still. My anxiety, I guess, is the continual fear of the unknown. And even as I write this, I am thinking "That's a silly statement, because No One Knows what tomorrow holds! Or even the next hour!" THEREFORE... I am reminding YOU, while I remind ME... that "God is our refuge and strength, an ever present help in trouble!!"] So, I pray that you will be very aware today that Our Lord is with you, just as He is with me! *Bonnie*

September 18

"Therefore, as God's chosen people, holy and dearly loved, clothe yourselves with compassion, kindness, humility, gentleness and patience. Bear with each other and forgive one another if any of you has a grievance against someone. Forgive as the Lord forgave you. And over all these virtues put on love, which binds them all together in perfect unity. Let the peace of Christ rule in your hearts, since as members of one body you were called to peace. And be thankful. Let the message of Christ dwell among you richly as you teach and admonish one another with all wisdom through psalms, hymns, and songs from the Spirit, singing to God with gratitude in your hearts. And whatever you do, whether in word or deed, do it all in the name of the Lord Jesus, giving thanks to God the Father through him."

Colossians 3:12-17 NIV

It's been a few months since I quoted these verses... they are such a beautiful reminder to me of how we should approach life! So, today... "whatever you do"... give Thanks to God the Father, in the name of the Lord Jesus!

Bonnie

""Come to me, all you who are weary and burdened, and I will give you rest. Take my yoke upon you and learn from me, for I am gentle and humble in heart, and you will find rest for your souls. For my yoke is easy and my burden is light.""

Matthew 11:28-30 NIV

Each time that I might start to think that I have difficult circumstances, or that my health issues make me feel weary, I try to remember: There are people in this world who truly have only 1 or 2 choices of what to wear today! There are some beggars on the streets who honestly do NOT have food to eat today. There are literally people in this world who have NEVER heard someone genuinely tell them, "I love you, and I care about your needs." .... Meanwhile, most of us have enjoyed ALL such blessings, and So Much More Besides!! THEREFORE, we should be EAGERLY sharing the Good News about Our Amazing Savior, Who is ready and willing to be their Savior too! And to support Missionaries who are spreading that Good News around the world! When I was halfway through 5th Grade, my three younger brothers and I got on a ship with my parents to travel to war-torn South Korea... going to tell them about Jesus. The three and a half years we spent there impacted my life forever! I witnessed genuine poverty and a war-torn land. Yet I also came to love worshiping with people who often shared generously from the little that they had in their own pockets. It is So Precious to Lean on Jesus!! HE alone truly Knows My Needs, and HE sacrificed His Own Life to save mine!! THEREFORE, I MUST Tell Others to Come to HIM! Because HE will Give You Rest!!

282.

Bonnie

September 20

"Keep on loving one another as brothers and sisters. Do not forget to show hospitality to strangers, for by so doing some people have shown hospitality to angels without knowing it. Continue to remember those in prison as if you were together with them in prison, and those who are mistreated as if you yourselves were suffering. Marriage should be honored by all, and the marriage bed kept pure, for God will judge the adulterer and all the sexually immoral. Keep your lives free from the love of money and be content with what you have, because God has said, "Never will I leave you; never will I forsake you." So we say with confidence, "The Lord is my helper; I will not be afraid. What can mere mortals do to me?" Remember your leaders, who spoke the word of God to you. Consider the outcome of their way of life and imitate their faith. Jesus Christ is the same yesterday and today and forever."

Hebrews 13:1-8 NIV

How reassuring that Our God cares about every part of our lives; and He urges us to encourage others.

Bonnie

September 21

"But God demonstrates his own love for us in this: While we were still sinners, Christ died for us."

Romans 5:8 NIV

— ◆·◆ —

This verse was shared by a dear friend who has eagerly shared this Good News with others at home and abroad... Bud and I were able to witness some of that mission work carried out in person, on our first trip together overseas. But we all know that we can also share that Good News right in our own neighborhood!!

Bonnie

September 22

"May God be gracious to us and bless us and make his face shine on us— so that your ways may be known on earth, your salvation among all nations. May the peoples praise you, God; may all the peoples praise you. May the nations be glad and sing for joy, for you rule the peoples with equity and guide the nations of the earth. May the peoples praise you, God; may all the peoples praise you. The land yields its harvest; God, our God, blesses us. May God bless us still, so that all the ends of the earth will fear him."

Psalms 67:1-7 NIV

Right here "down on the farm", I have a lovely view of a bountiful harvest, starting to be gathered.. and we Thank God for this blessing! .... How much MORE SO, we all need to be working diligently towards the Lord's "salvation among all nations" (as it says in verse 1)... Then... May ALL THE PEOPLES PRAISE YOU!!" Amen!!

Bonnie

285.

September 23

For God so loved the world that he gave his one and only Son, that whoever believes in him shall not perish but have eternal life. For God did not send his Son into the world to condemn the world, but to save the world through him. Whoever believes in him is not condemned, but whoever does not believe stands condemned already because they have not believed in the name of God's one and only Son. This is the verdict: Light has come into the world, but people loved darkness instead of light because their deeds were evil. Everyone who does evil hates the light, and will not come into the light for fear that their deeds will be exposed. But whoever lives by the truth comes into the light, so that it may be seen plainly that what they have done has been done in the sight of God."

John 3:16-21 NIV

As many of us have been sharing on Facebook about the blessings of our daughters and sons, these verses had a renewed impact on my thinking.... It is so hard to even fathom, but I believe with all my heart that these Words are Truth!

Bonnie

286.

September 24

"The LORD is my shepherd; I shall not want. He maketh me to lie down in green pastures: He leadeth me beside the still waters. He restoreth my soul: He leadeth me in the paths of righteousness for his name's sake. Yea, though I walk through the valley of the shadow of death, I will fear no evil: for thou art with me; Thy rod and thy staff they comfort me. Thou preparest a table before me in the presence of mine enemies: Thou anointest my head with oil; my cup runneth over. Surely goodness and mercy shall follow me all the days of my life: And I will dwell in the house of the LORD for ever."

Psalm 23:1-6 KJV

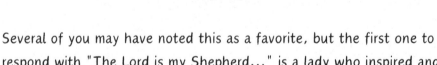

Several of you may have noted this as a favorite, but the first one to respond with "The Lord is my Shepherd..." is a lady who inspired and encouraged me the most in my career life, even to the point of challenging me to go back to school for my Master's Degree, and from there to another position with the State of Illinois. I will always be grateful for her influence in my life. I truly believe that Our Good Shepherd uses others to speak wisdom and encouragement into our lives.... if we will simply listen to His prompting.

Bonnie

September 25

"God opposes the proud but shows favor to the humble."
Humble yourselves, therefore, under God's mighty hand,
that he may lift you up in due time. Cast all your anxiety on
him because he cares for you."

1 Peter 5:5-7 NIV

It can give great comfort to cast all your anxiety on the Lord, and allow
HIM to handle it, and take control! HE is loving, and kind; and "HE
CARES!" ..... Thank You, Lord!!

Bonnie

September 26

"In you, Lord, I have taken refuge; let me never be put to shame. In your righteousness, rescue me and deliver me; turn your ear to me and save me. Be my rock of refuge, to which I can always go; give the command to save me, for you are my rock and my fortress. Deliver me, my God, from the hand of the wicked, from the grasp of those who are evil and cruel. For you have been my hope, Sovereign Lord, my confidence since my youth. From birth I have relied on you; you brought me forth from my mother's womb. I will ever praise you."

Psalms 71:1-6

How reassuring that God is our Refuge!!! Let's Praise Him today!!

Bonnie

September 27

"Who is wise and understanding among you? Let them show it by their good life, by deeds done in the humility that comes from wisdom. But if you harbor bitter envy and selfish ambition in your hearts, do not boast about it or deny the truth. Such "wisdom" does not come down from heaven but is earthly, unspiritual, demonic. For where you have envy and selfish ambition, there you find disorder and every evil practice. But the wisdom that comes from heaven is first of all pure; then peace-loving, considerate, submissive, full of mercy and good fruit, impartial and sincere. Peacemakers who sow in peace reap a harvest of righteousness."

James 3:13-18 NIV

Other than all of the writings of the Apostle John, the Letter from James is probably my favorite Epistle..... it is packed full of wisdom and practical advice, such as we see in these verses. So.... Here is what I did this morning... I read these verses aloud, as if they were Words of Advice, intended specifically for ME!.... which, of course, they WERE!! And For YOU Also.... So.... Now, it's your turn to read!

Bonnie

September 28

"When anxiety was great within me, Your consolation brought me joy."

Psalm 94:19

"Come near to God and He will come near to you. Wash your hands, you sinners, and purify your hearts, you double-minded."

James 4:8

These two verses truly spoke to my heart this morning, in the midst of this unusual season of my life; difficult to put into words, but in the midst of much confusion in my mind··· yet I am experiencing a true peace and contentment (most of the time); and I am convinced that this is true BECAUSE I have an amazing God, Who walks beside me, and gently guides me; AND He has blessed me with such a loving caring husband, and our wonderful attentive family!! ····. Having said that, I pray that these verses also speak to your heart today

Bonnie

September 29

But the fruit of the Spirit is love, joy, peace, patience, kindness, goodness, faithfulness, gentleness, self-control ; against such things there is no law.

Galatians 5:22

This was shared by a friend I met at Lincoln Christian College... she was assigned to be my "Big Sis" when she was a Sophomore and I was a Freshman at Lincoln Christian College (LBI back then). She would meet with me occasionally for devotions and prayer... and we would exchange notes of encouragement. After we both married and moved away from Lincoln, we lost track of each other for awhile.. then reconnected years later on, as she used to be from the Centralia area! Don't you love how God blesses us in ways we don't even imagine or anticipate?! HE is so good!!

Bonnie

September 30

"Let us not become weary in doing good, for at the proper time we will reap a harvest if we do not give up."

Galatians 6:9 NIV.

This great verse of encouragement was sent by a friend whose very life is an example of not giving up, despite her hardships or disappointments... and she finds many ways to "do good"... we can all be encouraged by this Scripture today!

Bonnie

293.

Bonnie and Bud with their children and their spouses.

October

October 1

"Who is wise and understanding among you? Let them show it by their good life, by deeds done in the humility that comes from wisdom. But if you harbor bitter envy and selfish ambition in your hearts, do not boast about it or deny the truth. Such "wisdom" does not come down from heaven but is earthly, unspiritual, demonic. For where you have envy and selfish ambition, there you find disorder and every evil practice. But the wisdom that comes from heaven is first of all pure; then peace-loving, considerate, submissive, full of mercy and good fruit, impartial and sincere. Peacemakers who sow in peace reap a harvest of righteousness."

James 3:13-18 NIV

Such positive advice that we each need to apply to our own lives... and encourage others to do the same!

295.

Bonnie

October 2

"Is anyone among you in trouble? Let them pray. Is anyone happy? Let them sing songs of praise. Is anyone among you sick? Let them call the elders of the church to pray over them and anoint them with oil in the name of the Lord. And the prayer offered in faith will make the sick person well; the Lord will raise them up. If they have sinned, they will be forgiven. Therefore confess your sins to each other and pray for each other so that you may be healed. The prayer of a righteous person is powerful and effective."

James 5:13-16 NIV

The God Who created you is listening! And HE Cares!! We are invited to lift up our Praises and Requests to HIM! ....HE IS LISTENING!

Bonnie

October 3

"Lord, hear my prayer, listen to my cry for mercy; in your faithfulness and righteousness come to my relief. Do not bring your servant into judgment, for no one living is righteous before you. The enemy pursues me, he crushes me to the ground; he makes me dwell in the darkness like those long dead. So my spirit grows faint within me; my heart within me is dismayed. I remember the days of long ago; I meditate on all your works and consider what your hands have done. I spread out my hands to you; I thirst for you like a parched land. Answer me quickly, Lord; my spirit fails. Do not hide your face from me or I will be like those who go down to the pit. Let the morning bring me word of your unfailing love, for I have put my trust in you. Show me the way I should go, for to you I entrust my life. Rescue me from my enemies, Lord, for I hide myself in you. Teach me to do your will, for you are my God; may your good Spirit lead me on level ground. For your name's sake, Lord, preserve my life; in your righteousness, bring me out of trouble. In your unfailing love, silence my enemies; destroy all my foes, for I am your servant."

Psalms 143:1-12 NIV

Before sharing this precious Psalm to you this morning, I literally read it aloud as my own prayer to Our Almighty God! And I invite you to do the same in your time of need.

Bonnie

October 4

"Paul then stood up in the meeting of the Areopagus and said: "People of Athens! I see that in every way you are very religious. For as I walked around and looked carefully at your objects of worship, I even found an altar with this inscription: to an unknown god. So you are ignorant of the very thing you worship—and this is what I am going to proclaim to you. "The God who made the world and everything in it is the Lord of heaven and earth and does not live in temples built by human hands. And he is not served by human hands, as if he needed anything. Rather, he himself gives everyone life and breath and everything else. From one man he made all the nations, that they should inhabit the whole earth; and he marked out their appointed times in history and the boundaries of their lands. God did this so that they would seek him and perhaps reach out for him and find him, though he is not far from any one of us. 'For in him we live and move and have our being.' As some of your own poets have said, 'We are his offspring.' "Therefore since we are God's offspring, we should not think that the divine being is like gold or silver or stone—an image made by human design and skill. In the past God overlooked such ignorance, but now he commands all people everywhere to repent. For he has set a day when he will judge the world with justice by the man he has appointed. He has given proof of this to everyone by raising him from the dead.""

Acts 17:22-31 NIV

AMEN!!! Friends, Let's live and act and speak up, and SHARE THIS GOOD NEWS! God sent His Only Son Jesus to be our Savior! Our Redeemer! And for This Good News, I am so grateful! *Bonnie*

298.

October 5

"Rejoice in the Lord always. I will say it again: Rejoice! Let your gentleness be evident to all. The Lord is near. Do not be anxious about anything, but in every situation, by prayer and petition, with thanksgiving, present your requests to God. And the peace of God, which transcends all understanding, will guard your hearts and your minds in Christ Jesus. Finally, brothers and sisters, whatever is true, whatever is noble, whatever is right, whatever is pure, whatever is lovely, whatever is admirable—if anything is excellent or praiseworthy—think about such things. Whatever you have learned or received or heard from me, or seen in me—put it into practice. And the God of peace will be with you."

Philippians 4:4-9 NIV

Dear Ones, I am well aware that I have shared these verses a few weeks ago... but they are sooo precious and meaningful to me and my current journey... so I am assuming that I am not alone in needing repeated REASSURANCE of the TRUTH that we hold as dear to our hearts... that we serve a LIVING GOD WHO CARES!!! So.... today, "in every situation"... give it all to HIM!!! And be blessed!! Amen!

Bonnie

October 6

"Praise be to the Lord, for he has heard my cry for mercy. The Lord is my strength and my shield; my heart trusts in him, and he helps me. My heart leaps for joy, and with my song I praise him. The Lord is the strength of his people, a fortress of salvation for his anointed one. Save your people and bless your inheritance; be their shepherd and carry them forever."

Psalms 28:6-9 NIV

Whatever is on your mind or in your heart today... whether troubling or joyous... give it all to The Lord, and let HIM be in control!! Then a genuine Peace can fill your mind and your day! ... Have a great weekend, and Worship Him with all your heart!!

Bonnie

300.

Bonnie's Blessings

October 7

"Though the fig tree does not bud and there are no grapes on the vines, though the olive crop fails and the fields produce no food, though there are no sheep in the pen and no cattle in the stalls, yet I will rejoice in the Lord, I will be joyful in God my Savior. The Sovereign Lord is my strength; He makes my feet like the feet of a deer, He enables me to tread on the heights."

Habakkuk 3:17-19 NIV

A very dear friend shared this passage with me many years ago, as we sat on bamboo furniture in her humble yet charming home in the heart of Africa! She pointed out that No Matter What our circumstances may be on any given day, we can still find reasons to Praise Our God!! This morning I am on my favorite comfy couch, looking out on lush fields which are yielding a bountiful harvest, and praising God for walking with us through good times as well as severe hardships! Also I thank Him for many friends who willingly face unknown peril to tell others of God's sacrificial love! And I promise Him that "even though" the harvest on our farm may not always be this plentiful "yet will we Praise Him!" And even though the mission of sharing the Gospel around the world may not always appear to be "bearing fruit" ··· yet we will Praise Him!! (Meanwhile there is NO excuse for failing to pray daily for those sharing God's Word near and far!

Bonnie

301.

October 8

"Have I not commanded you? Be strong and courageous. Do not be afraid; do not be discouraged, for the Lord your God will be with you wherever you go.""

Joshua 1:9 NIV

This is a timely reminder from a friend who has been thru many trials and setbacks, but learned to "not be afraid or discouraged."

Bonnie

October 9

"Trust in the Lord with all your heart and lean not on your own understanding; in all your ways submit to him, and he will make your paths straight. Do not be wise in your own eyes; fear the Lord and shun evil. This will bring health to your body and nourishment to your bones."

Proverbs 3:5-8 NIV

When I was in my early 40's my dear mother would have been in her 60's and she was teaching a Sunday School class of High School students! She was challenging them to memorize as many of The Proverbs as they could, so to be a good example she was preparing by memorizing this Proverb and others and quoting it to the class!! I reminded her that our brain cells don't work as well after our 50's and I think I hurt her feelings (which I never wanted to do!!) Now in my mid 70s I am content simply commit to READING all the Psalms and Proverbs!! Nevertheless, it is a valid goal to "hide His Word in our hearts!!

Bonnie

October 10

"But Jesus called the children to him and said, "Let the little children come to me, and do not hinder them, for the kingdom of God belongs to such as these. Truly I tell you, anyone who will not receive the kingdom of God like a little child will never enter it."

Luke 18:16-17 NIV

————— ✦•✦ —————

Probably the best example of obedience to these verses was my dear mother-in-law. Bud's mother lived out these words with dedicated passion. For decades she was one of the teachers in the Kindergarten Department of the Sunday School at Lincoln Christian Church. As each quarter in the curriculum approached, Hope and a friend would spend an entire Sunday afternoon organizing the printed lesson materials and flannel graph picture illustrations for each Sunday's lessons. It was truly a labor of love. Then on Sunday mornings I observed them welcoming each child to learn about the God Who loves them, and about His Son Jesus··· the One Who "loves the little children··· all the children of the world!" [Her name was Hope, and it was a fitting name for her. She taught her own sons well too!

Bonnie

The farmer sows the Word. Some people are like seed along the path, where the Word is sown. As soon as they hear it, Satan comes and takes away the Word that was sown in them. Others, like seed sown on rocky places, hear the Word and at once receive it with joy. But since they have no root, they last only a short time. When trouble or persecution comes because of the Word, they quickly fall away. Still others, like seed sown among thorns, hear the Word; but the worries of this life, the deceitfulness of wealth and the desires for other things come in and choke the Word, making it unfruitful. Others, like seed sown on good soil, hear the Word, accept it, and produce a crop—some thirty, some sixty, some a hundred times what was sown.""   Mark 4:14-20 NIV

This famous parable told by Jesus is even more effective if you start with verse 1 of the chapter.] That's the way my Dad would do it whenever he preached from the Gospels. I never got tired of hearing him do so! (And I would try to anticipate his next sentences.) Often we were traveling as he spoke at various churches; my brothers and I would try to guess which one of his sermons he was going to use that morning. This was one of my favorites... oh how I wish I could hear him preach again! (I have imagined that in Heaven we will have plenty of time to do so... although the real focus then will be praising the original Parable Teller!! The One Who died then rose again, so that we may be forgiven of our sins and be redeemed by His sacrifice for us!) Then we can spend all eternity praising Him together! That's what Joe Seggelke wanted to do... and now he is! Do you have a favorite Bible chapter, or recall a sermon you would enjoy hearing again, like reading a favorite story again and again? Or watching a favorite movie, even though you know the ending? God's Word tells us how to get ready for The Ending! We each need to obey His Word and be prepared! (That's what my Dad would tell you... "Get ready, because Jesus is Coming Again!"

Bonnie

October 12

"Better is one day in your courts than a thousand elsewhere; I would rather be a doorkeeper in the house of my God than dwell in the tents of the wicked. For the Lord God is a sun and shield; the Lord bestows favor and honor; no good thing does he withhold from those whose walk is blameless. Lord Almighty, blessed is the one who trusts in you."

Psalms 84:10-12 NIV

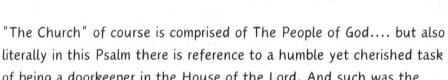

"The Church" of course is comprised of The People of God.... but also literally in this Psalm there is reference to a humble yet cherished task of being a doorkeeper in the House of the Lord. And such was the faithful duty of Wendell Charles Klockenga, Sr.... my Bud's dad. Wendell Sr was the greeter assigned to the door by the bell tower in the large church building at Lincoln Christian Church. If Wendell wasn't there on Sunday morning, he was either ill or visiting some of his grandchildren out of town! Wendell greeted people with a firm handshake and a smile, as his blue eyes sparkled! He loved others with a compassionate heart, but he loved God and his family first... Wow! How those blue eyes sparkled whenever one of his grandchildren were in the room!! I learned a lot over the years from Wendell, Sr. I learned about being dependable and caring and sincere. I learned about letting your light shine for Jesus by being a willing servant.

306.

Bonnie

October 13

"You, Lord, showed favor to your land; you restored the fortunes of Jacob. You forgave the iniquity of your people and covered all their sins. You set aside all your wrath and turned from your fierce anger. Restore us again, God our Savior, and put away your displeasure toward us. Will you be angry with us forever? Will you prolong your anger through all generations? Will you not revive us again, that your people may rejoice in you? Show us your unfailing love, Lord, and grant us your salvation. I will listen to what God the Lord says; he promises peace to his people, his faithful servants— but let them not turn to folly. Surely his salvation is near those who fear him, that his glory may dwell in our land. Love and faithfulness meet together; righteousness and peace kiss each other. Faithfulness springs forth from the earth, and righteousness looks down from heaven. The Lord will indeed give what is good, and our land will yield its harvest. Righteousness goes before him and prepares the way for his steps."

Psalms 85:1-13 NIV

Even as the farmers rejoice about a bountiful harvest.... let us eagerly "serve in His Fields" to help gather a great Harvest of Souls!" As the old hymn says: "We will come rejoicing, bringing in the sheaves!" Lord, help us stay focused on living our lives the Way You have taught in Your Word!!! And spread the Seed of the Gospel!!.... All Around the World!! REVIVE US AGAIN!!

Bonnie

October 14

"Lord, our Lord, how majestic is your name in all the earth!
You have set your glory in the heavens. Through the praise
of children and infants you have established a stronghold
against your enemies, to silence the foe and the avenger.
When I consider your heavens, the work of your fingers,
the moon and the stars, which you have set in place, what
is mankind that you are mindful of them, human beings
that you care for them?"

Psalms 8:1-4 NIV

Today, in our own family, we are having a special celebration, as our
first great-grandchild has turned one year old this month! Talk about
a precious reason to praise the Lord!! This is a very special JOY! . And
yet, so much greater still is the realization that our God gave His Only
Son to come to this earth as a sacrifice for sinners like you and me! (I
cannot even fathom the magnitude of His Love, Grace, and Mercy!!)
Be submissive to His Will and Praise Him today!   *Bonnie*

"I lift up my eyes to the mountains— where does my help come from? My help comes from the Lord, the Maker of heaven and earth. He will not let your foot slip— he who watches over you will not slumber; indeed, he who watches over Israel will neither slumber nor sleep. The Lord watches over you— the Lord is your shade at your right hand; the sun will not harm you by day, nor the moon by night. The Lord will keep you from all harm— he will watch over your life; the Lord will watch over your coming and going both now and forevermore."

Psalms 121:1-8 NIV

Good Morning; my message is a bit delayed since I spent the night at St Mary's Hospital at a pre-scheduled Sleep Apnea Testing. Years ago, I had to use a C-Pap Machine; then after I lost weight, the problem was not nearly as severe, and I was re-tested and allowed to go off of it. That was a huge relief!... Currently, with the extensive testing being done concerning my memory problems, one factor in question is whether or not I should actually return to using the BiPap machine. Studies have shown that the lack of sufficient oxygen to the brain can of course affect your thinking/and thus your memory. .... Compare this idea to when you feel really "groggy" if you don't get adequate sleep..... Anyway .... the only way to confirm that situation in my body, is to do this test. It is certainly NOT painful at all ... just awkward... and the staff at St Mary's is amazing! So.... it's done! And we will wait for the reports. However... Meanwhile.... I am taking my meds and keeping my follow-up appointments, and truly feeling GREAT!! I have more consultations coming up in the near future, and I continue to be so grateful for my amazing supportive family, and Our Great God!! Truth is, HE Watches Over each of us, and HE CARES!! Thank You, Lord!!

Bonnie

October 16

"The LORD is my shepherd; I shall not want. He maketh me to lie down in green pastures: He leadeth me beside the still waters. He restoreth my soul: He leadeth me in the paths of righteousness for his name's sake. Yea, though I walk through the valley of the shadow of death, I will fear no evil: for thou art with me; Thy rod and thy staff they comfort me. Thou preparest a table before me in the presence of mine enemies: Thou anointest my head with oil; my cup runneth over. Surely goodness and mercy shall follow me all the days of my life: And I will dwell in the house of the LORD for ever."

Psalm 23:1-6 KJV

I appreciate several various translations of this passage, I purposefully quote it on this Lord's Day in the King James Version... simply because that is how I memorized it as a young child, before the NIV was published.

310.

Bonnie

October 16

"Do not be deceived: God cannot be mocked. A man reaps what he sows. Whoever sows to please their flesh, from the flesh will reap destruction; whoever sows to please the Spirit, from the Spirit will reap eternal life. Let us not become weary in doing good, for at the proper time we will reap a harvest if we do not give up. Therefore, as we have opportunity, let us do good to all people, especially to those who belong to the family of believers."

Galatians 6:7-10 NIV

Obviously, as the wife of a farmer, "HARVEST" is a very important word..... all the hard work leading up to that time, hopefully results in an abundance of grain (or whatever else was planted.) The same is true of our words and actions! What are we "sowing"?? What are we "spreading around" by the way we live our lives, and by our choices? What are our priorities?? The people around us are watching and listening!! What are they learning about us? More importantly: What are they learning about Our God??!! The world needs to know that The One True God is a God Who Saves! The God Who Loves! The God Who offers Redemption and Eternal Life!! Let's be diligent about sowing that seed! The Harvest is upon us!! Praise HIM! Bonnie

October 17

"I remember my affliction and my wandering, the bitterness and the gall. I well remember them, and my soul is downcast within me. Yet this I call to mind and therefore I have hope: Because of the Lord's great love we are not consumed, for his compassions never fail. They are new every morning; great is your faithfulness. I say to myself, "The Lord is my portion; therefore I will wait for him." The Lord is good to those whose hope is in him, to the one who seeks him; it is good to wait quietly for the salvation of the Lord. It is good for a man to bear the yoke while he is young."

Lamentations 3:19-27

This is one of my "No Matter What" references··· because··· no matter what I am going through··· someone has definitely experienced worse times than I have! But mostly because "The Lord is my portion" and HE IS FAITHFUL!!

Bonnie

Bonnie's Blessings

October 18

"But whatever were gains to me I now consider loss for the sake of Christ. What is more, I consider everything a loss because of the surpassing worth of knowing Christ Jesus my Lord, for whose sake I have lost all things. I consider them garbage, that I may gain Christ and be found in him, not having a righteousness of my own that comes from the law, but that which is through faith in Christ—the righteousness that comes from God on the basis of faith. I want to know Christ—yes, to know the power of his resurrection and participation in his sufferings, becoming like him in his death, and so, somehow, attaining to the resurrection from the dead. Not that I have already obtained all this, or have already arrived at my goal, but I press on to take hold of that for which Christ Jesus took hold of me. Brothers and sisters, I do not consider myself yet to have taken hold of it. But one thing I do: Forgetting what is behind and straining toward what is ahead, I press on toward the goal to win the prize for which God has called me heavenward in Christ Jesus."
Philippians 3:7-14 NIV

Friends, over the years Bud and I... plus MANY of you... have been able to follow Chuck Melton and his amazing teammates, as they have worked so hard at their sport, forming the dynamic USA Wheelchair Rugby Team ... and yesterday they won the Silver Trophy in Worldwide competition!!! So proud and excited for them!!! .... Now, Re-Read those verses above, and consider how diligently each of us should be working hard to serve Our Lord, and share the Good News of Christ and His Salvation!!! ... "Pressing on toward the goal to win the prize for which God has called me heavenward in Christ Jesus!" PRESS ON!!!

Bonnie

313.

October 19

"Search me, God, and know my heart; test me and know my anxious thoughts. See if there is any offensive way in me, and lead me in the way everlasting."

Psalms 139:23-24 NIV

———◆·◆———

Precious Words of submission as we worship our Savior today!

Bonnie

October 20

"Dear friends, let us love one another, for love comes from God. Everyone who loves has been born of God and knows God. Whoever does not love does not know God, because God is love. This is how God showed his love among us: He sent his one and only Son into the world that we might live through him. This is love: not that we loved God, but that he loved us and sent his Son as an atoning sacrifice for our sins."

1 John 4:7-10 NIV

This beautiful passage is a great reminder that our lives... our thoughts and attitudes and actions... should demonstrate our love for others. And it's not a contest as to who can do it best; it should be our way of life. Our love for God should be obvious to others, by the way we treat them, thus demonstrating our love for them also! .... And that is NOT always easy, unless I let God control my thoughts and attitude!! Because "LOVE COMES FROM GOD." (Read the first sentence of this Scripture again!)

Bonnie

315.

"Turn from evil and do good; seek peace and pursue it. The eyes of the Lord are on the righteous, and his ears are attentive to their cry; but the face of the Lord is against those who do evil, to blot out their name from the earth. The righteous cry out, and the Lord hears them; he delivers them from all their troubles. The Lord is close to the brokenhearted and saves those who are crushed in spirit. The righteous person may have many troubles, but the Lord delivers him from them all; he protects all his bones, not one of them will be broken. Evil will slay the wicked; the foes of the righteous will be condemned. The Lord will rescue his servants; no one who takes refuge in him will be condemned."

Psalms 34:14-22 NIV

This is such a beautiful Psalm! Reassuring··· in "good times or bad times" ····.because we can ALWAYS "take refuge in HIM" . Therefore, lean on HIM today!

Bonnie

October 21

"In you, Lord, I have taken refuge; let me never be put to shame. In your righteousness, rescue me and deliver me; turn your ear to me and save me. Be my rock of refuge, to which I can always go; give the command to save me, for you are my rock and my fortress. Deliver me, my God, from the hand of the wicked, from the grasp of those who are evil and cruel. For you have been my hope, Sovereign Lord, my confidence since my youth. From birth I have relied on you; you brought me forth from my mother's womb. I will ever praise you."

Psalms 71:1-6 NIV

———— ✦·✦ ————

Even though you and I have not endured exactly the same trauma that this Psalm writer had experienced···. Still these Words spoke to my heart today··· and I pray that you also are reminded that Our God is Faithful!!

Bonnie

"Keep on loving one another as brothers and sisters. Do not forget to show hospitality to strangers, for by so doing some people have shown hospitality to angels without knowing it. Continue to remember those in prison as if you were together with them in prison, and those who are mistreated as if you yourselves were suffering. Marriage should be honored by all, and the marriage bed kept pure, for God will judge the adulterer and all the sexually immoral. Keep your lives free from the love of money and be content with what you have, because God has said, "Never will I leave you; never will I forsake you." So we say with confidence, "The Lord is my helper; I will not be afraid. What can mere mortals do to me?" Remember your leaders, who spoke the word of God to you. Consider the outcome of their way of life and imitate their faith. Jesus Christ is the same yesterday and today and forever."

Hebrews 13:1-8 NIV

Dynamic challenging and encouraging verses as we close out this week! Our Lord truly cares about every aspect of our lives! Our motives, thoughts, and actions need to be submitted to HIS WAY! Only then can we find genuine Peace in our hearts and minds! THANK YOU, LORD for providing a way!!

Bonnie

318.

October 23

"May our Lord Jesus Christ himself and God our Father, who loved us and by his grace gave us eternal encouragement and good hope, encourage your hearts and strengthen you in every good deed and word."

2 Thessalonians 2:16-17 NIV

Praying that we may focus on the blessing of the Good News of Jesus. Then allow that focus to influence every choice and decision that we make.

Bonnie

October 24

"After John was put in prison, Jesus went into Galilee, proclaiming the good news of God. "The time has come," he said. "The kingdom of God has come near. Repent and believe the good news!" As Jesus walked beside the Sea of Galilee, he saw Simon and his brother Andrew casting a net into the lake, for they were fishermen. "Come, follow me," Jesus said, "and I will send you out to fish for people." At once they left their nets and followed him."

Mark 1:14-18 NIV

My prayer today is that each of us would always be so eager to share The Good News of Jesus and the Redemption that can only come through Him!

Bonnie

October 25

"For the message of the cross is foolishness to those who are perishing, but to us who are being saved it is the power of God. For it is written: "I will destroy the wisdom of the wise; the intelligence of the intelligent I will frustrate.""

1 Corinthians 1:18-19 NIV

Praise God for "The Message of The Cross" which provides for us the path to Redemption and New Life through Christ Jesus, Our Lord!

321.

Bonnie

October 26

"In the beginning was the Word, and the Word was with God, and the Word was God. He was with God in the beginning. Through him all things were made; without him nothing was made that has been made. In him was life, and that life was the light of all mankind. The light shines in the darkness, and the darkness has not overcome it. There was a man sent from God whose name was John. He came as a witness to testify concerning that light, so that through him all might believe. He himself was not the light; he came only as a witness to the light. The true light that gives light to everyone was coming into the world. He was in the world, and though the world was made through him, the world did not recognize him. He came to that which was his own, but his own did not receive him. Yet to all who did receive him, to those who believed in his name, he gave the right to become children of God— children born not of natural descent, nor of human decision or a husband's will, but born of God. The Word became flesh and made his dwelling among us. We have seen his glory, the glory of the one and only Son, who came from the Father, full of grace and truth."

John 1:1-14 NIV

———— ✦•✦ ————

[Thanking The Lord this day for His Truth and Light, which gives Hope and Grace and Peace and Purpose to each day of our lives.

Bonnie

October 27

"Jesus went through all the towns and villages, teaching in their synagogues, proclaiming the good news of the kingdom and healing every disease and sickness. When he saw the crowds, he had compassion on them, because they were harassed and helpless, like sheep without a shepherd. Then he said to his disciples, "The harvest is plentiful but the workers are few. Ask the Lord of the harvest, therefore, to send out workers into his harvest field.""

Matthew 9:35-38 NIV

—◆·◆—

Let us be found eagerly sharing The Good News and rejoice in the Harvest of Souls!

Bonnie

October 28

"But the wisdom that comes from heaven is first of all pure; then peace-loving, considerate, submissive, full of mercy and good fruit, impartial and sincere. Peacemakers who sow in peace reap a harvest of righteousness."

James 3:17-18 NIV

Such a dynamic description of how we should live and act each day! Let us each seek to be Peacemakers!

324.

Bonnie

October 29

"For I am not ashamed of the gospel, because it is the power of God that brings salvation to everyone who believes: first to the Jew, then to the Gentile. For in the gospel the righteousness of God is revealed—a righteousness that is by faith from first to last, just as it is written: "The righteous will live by faith.""

Romans 1:16-17 NIV

Praying today that God will give each of us the desire to eagerly share the Good News of the salvation He offers to all who will believe and obey!

Bonnie

October 30

"As for me, I will always have hope; I will praise you more and more. My mouth will tell of your righteous deeds, of your saving acts all day long— though I know not how to relate them all. I will come and proclaim your mighty acts, Sovereign Lord; I will proclaim your righteous deeds, yours alone. Since my youth, God, you have taught me, and to this day I declare your marvelous deeds. Even when I am old and gray, do not forsake me, my God, till I declare your power to the next generation, your mighty acts to all who are to come."

Psalms 71:14-18 NIV

Oh, how I long for these verses to describe my life! Friends, our words and actions need to declare to the next generation that we worship a powerful God Who is full of Love!!

Bonnie

October 31

"But, dear friends, remember what the apostles of our Lord Jesus Christ foretold. They said to you, "In the last times there will be scoffers who will follow their own ungodly desires." These are the people who divide you, who follow mere natural instincts and do not have the Spirit. But you, dear friends, by building yourselves up in your most holy faith and praying in the Holy Spirit, keep yourselves in God's love as you wait for the mercy of our Lord Jesus Christ to bring you to eternal life. Be merciful to those who doubt; save others by snatching them from the fire; to others show mercy, mixed with fear—hating even the clothing stained by corrupted flesh. To him who is able to keep you from stumbling and to present you before his glorious presence without fault and with great joy— to the only God our Savior be glory, majesty, power and authority, through Jesus Christ our Lord, before all ages, now and forevermore! Amen."

Jude 1:17-25 NIV

———— ✦·✦ ————

This Epistle is just one chapter long; it's a good read to start the week.

 "To the only God our Savior be glory, majesty, power and authority, through Jesus Christ our Lord, before all ages, now and forever! Amen!!"

Bonnie

November

November 1

"Remind the people to be subject to rulers and authorities, to be obedient, to be ready to do whatever is good, to slander no one, to be peaceable and considerate, and always to be gentle toward everyone. At one time we too were foolish, disobedient, deceived and enslaved by all kinds of passions and pleasures. We lived in malice and envy, being hated and hating one another. But when the kindness and love of God our Savior appeared, he saved us, not because of righteous things we had done, but because of his mercy. He saved us through the washing of rebirth and renewal by the Holy Spirit, whom he poured out on us generously through Jesus Christ our Savior, so that, having been justified by his grace, we might become heirs having the hope of eternal life. This is a trustworthy saying. And I want you to stress these things, so that those who have trusted in God may be careful to devote themselves to doing what is good. These things are excellent and profitable for everyone."

Titus 3:1-8 NIV

—◆•◆—

This letter is full of practical advice about our attitude and choices in our Christian walk··· it's good to read the whole book, and take it to heart, as we "devote ourselves to doing what is good."

Bonnie

November 2

"You will keep in perfect peace those whose minds are steadfast, because they trust in you. Trust in the Lord forever, for the Lord, the Lord himself, is the Rock eternal."

Isaiah 26:3-4 NIV

It truly is so good and sweet to Trust in Jesus!! Literally all my life I have been surrounded by people who were a living example of such trusting, and now I claim it for me own foundation and way of life. Praying that all others would know the same peace of mind and heart.

Bonnie

November 3

"Now we ask you, brothers and sisters, to acknowledge those who work hard among you, who care for you in the Lord and who admonish you. Hold them in the highest regard in love because of their work. Live in peace with each other. And we urge you, brothers and sisters, warn those who are idle and disruptive, encourage the disheartened, help the weak, be patient with everyone. Make sure that nobody pays back wrong for wrong, but always strive to do what is good for each other and for everyone else. pray continually, give thanks in all circumstances; for this is God's will for you in Christ Jesus. Do not quench the Spirit. Do not treat prophecies with contempt but test them all; hold on to what is good, reject every kind of evil. May God himself, the God of peace, sanctify you through and through. May your whole spirit, soul and body be kept blameless at the coming of our Lord Jesus Christ. The one who calls you is faithful, and he will do it."

1 Thessalonians 5:12-15, 17-24 NIV.

Dear Ones, These verses are shared as we approach the weekend. Let's each make a special effort to express our appreciation to those who "work hard among us" in sharing the Gospel and God's Love!

Bonnie

331.

November 4

"For I know the plans I have for you," declares the Lord, "plans to prosper you and not to harm you, plans to give you hope and a future. Then you will call on me and come and pray to me, and I will listen to you. You will seek me and find me when you seek me with all your heart."

Jeremiah 29:11-13 NIV

My prayer today: "Lord, please continue to give me hope and a future; Thank You for guiding me!" Amen

Bonnie

November 5

"You are righteous, Lord, and your laws are right. The statutes you have laid down are righteous; they are fully trustworthy. My zeal wears me out, for my enemies ignore your words. Your promises have been thoroughly tested, and your servant loves them. Though I am lowly and despised, I do not forget your precepts. Your righteousness is everlasting and your law is true. Trouble and distress have come upon me, but your commands give me delight. Your statutes are always righteous; give me understanding that I may live. I call with all my heart; answer me, Lord, and I will obey your decrees."

Psalms 119:137-145 NIV

Call to Him "with all your heart" today!

333.

Bonnie

November 6

"Do not be deceived: God cannot be mocked. A man reaps what he sows. Whoever sows to please their flesh, from the flesh will reap destruction; whoever sows to please the Spirit, from the Spirit will reap eternal life. Let us not become weary in doing good, for at the proper time we will reap a harvest if we do not give up. Therefore, as we have opportunity, let us do good to all people, especially to those who belong to the family of believers."

Galatians 6:7-10 NIV

Here on the farm, the focus is on a good harvest; MUCH effort and planning goes into the work, and much rejoicing when the harvest is bountiful. How much more so, should be our efforts to plant the seed of the Gospel! The Good News that God has provided a Savior! "Let us not become weary!" Let us eagerly share the Good News!!

Bonnie

November 7

"Rejoice in the Lord always. I will say it again: Rejoice! Let your gentleness be evident to all. The Lord is near. Do not be anxious about anything, but in every situation, by prayer and petition, with thanksgiving, present your requests to God. And the peace of God, which transcends all understanding, will guard your hearts and your minds in Christ Jesus. Finally, brothers and sisters, whatever is true, whatever is noble, whatever is right, whatever is pure, whatever is lovely, whatever is admirable—if anything is excellent or praiseworthy—think about such things. Whatever you have learned or received or heard from me, or seen in me—put it into practice. And the God of peace will be with you."

Philippians 4:4-9 NIV

Sharing this today as a reminder and reassurance which I need··· so I figured that perhaps you need this also! These days can become so cluttered and busy··· some of that is good of course, but much is just non-essential in the light of this list: "Noble, Right, Pure, Lovely, Admirable, Excellent, Praiseworthy" ··· So today let's focus more on "such things" as these!   335.   Bonnie

November 8

"Trust in the Lord with all your heart and lean not on your own understanding; in all your ways submit to him, and he will make your paths straight."

Proverbs 3:5-6 NIV

Both in the difficult days, and the delightful occasions... These Words from The Lord ring True!!

336.

Bonnie

November 9

"May the God of hope fill you with all joy and peace as you trust in him, so that you may overflow with hope by the power of the Holy Spirit."

Romans 15:13 NIV

Praying that your day··· indeed you week··· would be filled with

"Hope and Joy and Peace" , which can indeed be found in Jesus!

Bonnie

337.

November 10

"For I know the plans I have for you," declares the Lord, "plans to prosper you and not to harm you, plans to give you hope and a future. Then you will call on me and come and pray to me, and I will listen to you. You will seek me and find me when you seek me with all your heart."

Jeremiah 29:11-13 NIV

Leaning on these precious favorites today, and finding them ALWAYS to be true!! Thank You, Lord!

Bonnie

November 11

"The Lord is my shepherd, I lack nothing. He makes me lie down in green pastures, he leads me beside quiet waters, he refreshes my soul. He guides me along the right paths for his name's sake. Even though I walk through the darkest valley, I will fear no evil, for you are with me; your rod and your staff, they comfort me. You prepare a table before me in the presence of my enemies. You anoint my head with oil; my cup overflows. Surely your goodness and love will follow me all the days of my life, and I will dwell in the house of the Lord forever."

Psalms 23:1-6 NIV

———— ◆·◆ ————

This well-known Psalm I have shared before in KJV but today I am sharing it from the NIV especially for a friend who has been in the hospital, and she treasures these Words.

339.

Bonnie

"I thank my God every time I remember you. In all my prayers for all of you, I always pray with joy because of your partnership in the gospel from the first day until now, being confident of this, that he who began a good work in you will carry it on to completion until the day of Christ Jesus. It is right for me to feel this way about all of you, since I have you in my heart and, whether I am in chains or defending and confirming the gospel, all of you share in God's grace with me. God can testify how I long for all of you with the affection of Christ Jesus. And this is my prayer: that your love may abound more and more in knowledge and depth of insight, so that you may be able to discern what is best and may be pure and blameless for the day of Christ, filled with the fruit of righteousness that comes through Jesus Christ—to the glory and praise of God."

Philippians 1:3-11 NIV

What a great God we serve! Headed now to Branson with my Bud! Love these special getaways with him! Feeling blessed! Hope you have a great day.

Bonnie

November 13

"We wait in hope for the Lord; he is our help and our shield. In him our hearts rejoice, for we trust in his holy name. May your unfailing love be with us, Lord, even as we put our hope in you."

Psalms 33:20-22 NIV

— ◆·◆ —

Praying this morning that you take comfort in this verse, just as I have this morning. Our God hears our prayers, and HE Cares! Let us put our Hope in HIM.

Bonnie

Bonnie's Blessings

"There is a time for everything, and a season for every activity under the heavens: a time to be born and a time to die, a time to plant and a time to uproot, a time to kill and a time to heal, a time to tear down and a time to build, a time to weep and a time to laugh, a time to mourn and a time to dance, a time to scatter stones and a time to gather them, a time to embrace and a time to refrain from embracing, a time to search and a time to give up, a time to keep and a time to throw away, a time to tear and a time to mend, a time to be silent and a time to speak, a time to love and a time to hate, a time for war and a time for peace. What do workers gain from their toil? I have seen the burden God has laid on the human race. He has made everything beautiful in its time. He has also set eternity in the human heart; yet no one can fathom what God has done from beginning to end. I know that there is nothing better for people than to be happy and to do good while they live. That each of them may eat and drink, and find satisfaction in all their toil—this is the gift of God. I know that everything God does will endure forever; nothing can be added to it and nothing taken from it. God does it so that people will fear him."

Ecclesiastes 3:1-14 NIV

This is a week of "contemplation" for me... how about you? It is good to review all God has done for you, and what He has brought you through. At the same time, we can open our hearts to Him about whatever might be ahead for us. Lean on Him... Always!! No Matter What!

Bonnie

November 15

"Rejoice in the Lord always. I will say it again: Rejoice! Let your gentleness be evident to all. The Lord is near. Do not be anxious about anything, but in every situation, by prayer and petition, with thanksgiving, present your requests to God. And the peace of God, which transcends all understanding, will guard your hearts and your minds in Christ Jesus. Finally, brothers and sisters, whatever is true, whatever is noble, whatever is right, whatever is pure, whatever is lovely, whatever is admirable—if anything is excellent or praiseworthy—think about such things."

Philippians 4:4-8 NIV

As we approach this Thanksgiving time in America, I am reminded that we all have so much to be thankful for... No Matter how much or how little we possess in earthly things...we ALL can be Thankful for the Love and Sacrifice our Lord provides for all who will accept Him! There is No Greater Blessing!

343.

Bonnie

November 16

"Let love and faithfulness never leave you; bind them around your neck, write them on the tablet of your heart. Then you will win favor and a good name in the sight of God and man. Trust in the Lord with all your heart and lean not on your own understanding; in all your ways submit to him, and he will make your paths straight."

Proverbs 3:3-6 NIV

Praying that you have a blessed day, as we put this advice into practice in our daily lives.

Bonnie

Bonnie's Blessings

"Now we ask you, brothers and sisters, to acknowledge those who work hard among you, who care for you in the Lord and who admonish you. Hold them in the highest regard in love because of their work. Live in peace with each other. And we urge you, brothers and sisters, warn those who are idle and disruptive, encourage the disheartened, help the weak, be patient with everyone. Make sure that nobody pays back wrong for wrong, but always strive to do what is good for each other and for everyone else. Rejoice always, pray continually, give thanks in all circumstances; for this is God's will for you in Christ Jesus."

1 Thessalonians 5:12-18 NIV.

Some years, while approaching Thanksgiving Day, I have started a written list of "Things I am Thankful for"... and it never took long before I realized: "It's not about the THINGS!" It's about a loving God; it's about His Saving Grace; it's about the love of Family and Friends; it's about the joy and privilege of Worshipping Our Lord and Savior! It's about His Eternal Love! Let's fill our hearts and minds with Giving Thanks!

Bonnie

345.

November 17

"Therefore, as God's chosen people, holy and dearly loved, clothe yourselves with compassion, kindness, humility, gentleness and patience. Bear with each other and forgive one another if any of you has a grievance against someone. Forgive as the Lord forgave you. And over all these virtues put on love, which binds them all together in perfect unity. Let the peace of Christ rule in your hearts, since as members of one body you were called to peace. And be thankful. Let the message of Christ dwell among you richly as you teach and admonish one another with all wisdom through psalms, hymns, and songs from the Spirit, singing to God with gratitude in your hearts. And whatever you do, whether in word or deed, do it all in the name of the Lord Jesus, giving thanks to God the Father through him."

Colossians 3:12-17 NIV

More beautiful Words to remind us to "Give Thanks!"

Bonnie

November 18

I know what it is to be in need, and I know what it is to have plenty. I have learned the secret of being content in any and every situation, whether well fed or hungry, whether living in plenty or in want. I can do all this through him who gives me strength."

Philippians 4:12-13 NIV

No Matter What your circumstances may be today.... The Lord Cares!! HE can provide the strength you need right now. Cast all your anxiety on Him, and He will Lift you up!!

Bonnie

November 19

"Then the eleven disciples went to Galilee, to the mountain where Jesus had told them to go. When they saw him, they worshiped him; but some doubted. Then Jesus came to them and said, "All authority in heaven and on earth has been given to me. Therefore go and make disciples of all nations, baptizing them in the name of the Father and of the Son and of the Holy Spirit, and teaching them to obey everything I have commanded you. And surely I am with you always, to the very end of the age.""

Matthew 28:16-20 NIV

❖·❖

Today, let us draw Strength and Reassurance from these Words of Truth!

Bonnie

348.

November 20

"There is a time for everything, and a season for every activity under the heavens: a time to be born and a time to die, a time to plant and a time to uproot, a time to kill and a time to heal, a time to tear down and a time to build, a time to weep and a time to laugh, a time to mourn and a time to dance, a time to scatter stones and a time to gather them, a time to embrace and a time to refrain from embracing, a time to search and a time to give up, a time to keep and a time to throw away, a time to tear and a time to mend, a time to be silent and a time to speak, a time to love and a time to hate, a time for war and a time for peace. What do workers gain from their toil? I have seen the burden God has laid on the human race. He has made everything beautiful in its time. He has also set eternity in the human heart; yet no one can fathom what God has done from beginning to end. I know that there is nothing better for people than to be happy and to do good while they live. That each of them may eat and drink, and find satisfaction in all their toil—this is the gift of God.

Ecclesiastes 3:1-13 NIV

While these amazing thoughts are deep and beautiful and meaningful··· We can today rejoice that Because of Christ and His Sacrifice··· Life DOES have MEANING, and we CAN. claim God's offer and promises of salvation and of eternity with Him! ··· So it is my prayer today that we each would find our days to Be MEANINGFUL, as we focus of HIS BLESSINGS of Hope and Salvation!!] Have a great weekend, remembering to spend time in His Word, and in serving others!

Bonnie

Bud's Chocolate Chip Cookies

This is the story of the Klockenga Chocolate Chip Cookie Tradition.

Bud and I started dating during our high school years, although we attended different schools so we mostly were together at church youth activities, plus occasional dates and family events. After we had dated a couple years, occasionally Bud would come to the Seggelke house for a visit and we would work on our homework assignments; sometimes I would type papers he had written, once he started college.

Early on, it was clear that he loved chocolate, and especially chocolate chip cookies. So, one study night, I baked chocolate chip cookies for him. After this had become a regular habit, one evening he held up his cookie and declared: "I bet I could eat more of your chocolate chip cookies in a lifetime than you could bake for me!"

He later said that was his first proposal to me! I gladly accepted the challenge.

We held true to the promise to the extent that I packed chocolate chip cookies in my suitcase when we went on our honeymoon. And then, we made sure each time we got groceries that we had the chips and other ingredients on hand.

This soon became a well-known fact, and everyone expected chocolate chip cookies when they came to the Klockenga house. Our children have always had them available. At times, due to budget and dieting concerns, we tried to limit the number of cookies consumed in a day or week, but nevertheless, the baking continued...... 350.

Bonnie's Blessings

Eventually, we expanded this to sending cookies to servicemen overseas. Also we enjoyed packing them with us when we visited missionaries on the field overseas. When we visited the orphanage in India, we packed chocolate chips and several other ingredients in our luggage; the onsite bakery at the orphanage had the other basic ingredients. We had so much fun passing out the cookies to the students as they arrived home from school that first baking day. We soon learned that some of them had literally never tasted chocolate before!

I used the recipe on the back of the Nestle Toll House Chocolate Chip package. However, I often do not carefully measure the sugar, brown sugar, or chocolate chips. Instead, I often dump in extra of each. Also, it varies how large I make the cookies. Our grown children have all carried on the tradition, often baking chocolate chip cookies in their own homes, although they each have come up with their own variations of the recipe. Since we have been married over 55 years, I have not actually calculated how many cookies we have actually baked. But to this day, we have always had some available in our home. It has been lots of fun.

November 21

"I will give thanks to the Lord because of his righteousness;
I will sing the praises of the name of the Lord Most High."

Psalms 7:17 NIV

Also, please read these prayers of thanksgiving from the Psalms: 9:1,
35:18, 69:30, 95:2, 100:4, 106:1, 119:62. Each none of these verses
blessed my heart today, and I pray you will be blessed also! Praying
that your heart will be overflowing with gratitude for all God's
Blessings! May the Lord bless you!!

352.

Bonnie

November 22

""But to you who are listening I say: Love your enemies, do good to those who hate you, bless those who curse you, pray for those who mistreat you. If someone slaps you on one cheek, turn to them the other also. If someone takes your coat, do not withhold your shirt from them. Give to everyone who asks you, and if anyone takes what belongs to you, do not demand it back. Do to others as you would have them do to you."

Luke 6:27-31 NIV

Wow!! I am sure that I do not consistently display an attitude this generous, to all people! I've got some work to do! How about you?

Bonnie

"Do not conform to the pattern of this world, but be transformed by the renewing of your mind. Then you will be able to test and approve what God's will is—his good, pleasing and perfect will."

Romans 12:2 NIV

"For the Spirit God gave us does not make us timid, but gives us power, love and self-discipline."

2 Timothy 1:7 NIV...

Especially in my "retirement years" I find myself more prone to easily wasting my time and energy doing pointless things, or wasting time when in fact there is a long "To Do List" laying on the table, and I know that I should be reaching out to help others who are in need. Truth is, that each of us need to consider our priorities and ask The Lord for Wisdom as we make our choices. Let's Trust HIM today, to "give us power and love and self-discipline"!

Bonnie

November 24

""For through the law I died to the law so that I might live for God. I have been crucified with Christ and I no longer live, but Christ lives in me. The life I now live in the body, I live by faith in the Son of God, who loved me and gave himself for me. I do not set aside the grace of God, for if righteousness could be gained through the law, Christ died for nothing!""

Galatians 2:19-21 NIV

Praise God for the indescribable gift of His Son!

355.

Bonnie

November 25

"Though the fig tree does not bud and there are no grapes on the vines, though the olive crop fails and the fields produce no food, though there are no sheep in the pen and no cattle in the stalls, yet I will rejoice in the Lord, I will be joyful in God my Savior. The Sovereign Lord is my strength; he makes my feet like the feet of a deer, he enables me to tread on the heights. For the director of music. On my stringed instruments."

Habakkuk 3:17-19 NIV

It is so easy to sing praises and be glad, when it seems "everything is going our way" However, we worship and serve a God Who knows and cares about the deepest needs of our hearts and minds! How precious it is to be able to declare: "The Sovereign Lord is my strength!"

Bonnie

November 26

"Sing the praises of the Lord, you his faithful people; praise his holy name. For his anger lasts only a moment, but his favor lasts a lifetime; weeping may stay for the night, but rejoicing comes in the morning."

Psalms 30:4-5 NIV

— ❧·❧ —

Somehow, I never tire of this reminder! In times of joy or sorrow, HE is Always FAITHFUL!

357.

Bonnie

November 27

"Sing the praises of the Lord, you his faithful people; praise his holy name. For his anger lasts only a moment, but his favor lasts a lifetime; weeping may stay for the night, but rejoicing comes in the morning."

Psalms 30:4-5 NIV

———— ✦·✦ ————

Somehow, I never tire of this reminder! In times of joy or sorrow, HE is Always FAITHFUL!

358.

Bonnie

November 27

"For this God is our God for ever and ever; He will be our guide even to the end."

Psalms 48:14 NIV

This morning, this verse was posted on FB by a friend on the other side of the world, written in her native language; I had to look up the translation. However, one glorious day we will bow down before The Throne together, and none of us will need an interpreter as we Worship and Praise Our God with one voice!

Bonnie

"Do not fret because of those who are evil or be envious of those who do wrong; for like the grass they will soon wither, like green plants they will soon die away. Trust in the Lord and do good; dwell in the land and enjoy safe pasture. Take delight in the Lord, and he will give you the desires of your heart. Commit your way to the Lord; trust in him and he will do this: He will make your righteous reward shine like the dawn, your vindication like the noonday sun. Be still before the Lord and wait patiently for him; do not fret when people succeed in their ways, when they carry out their wicked schemes. Refrain from anger and turn from wrath; do not fret—it leads only to evil.

Psalms 37:1-8 NIV

It would certainly not be accurate to claim that I "never fret!" However, throughput my life, it has proven evident time and time again that we can Trust in The Lord, and we Can Find REFUGE In HIM!! So I am praying that you have that same peace and reassurance in your heart and mind, as this Psalm portrays.

Bonnie

November 29

"You were taught, with regard to your former way of life, to put off your old self, which is being corrupted by its deceitful desires; to be made new in the attitude of your minds; and to put on the new self, created to be like God in true righteousness and holiness. Therefore each of you must put off falsehood and speak truthfully to your neighbor, for we are all members of one body. "In your anger do not sin": Do not let the sun go down while you are still angry, and do not give the devil a foothold. Anyone who has been stealing must steal no longer, but must work, doing something useful with their own hands, that they may have something to share with those in need. Do not let any unwholesome talk come out of your mouths, but only what is helpful for building others up according to their needs, that it may benefit those who listen. And do not grieve the Holy Spirit of God, with whom you were sealed for the day of redemption. Get rid of all bitterness, rage and anger, brawling and slander, along with every form of malice. Be kind and compassionate[to one another, forgiving each other, just as in Christ God forgave you."

Ephesians 4:22-32 NIV

This wise counsel, written by the Apostle Paul centuries ago, still applies to us today. Too often, angry words are not only spoken in private, but even plastered all over Facebook and other media. It is my prayer that we would each make a concerted effort to be a good example to others, of how to be "kind and compassionate, and forgiving!"

Bonnie

November 30

""Come to me, all you who are weary and burdened, and I will give you rest. Take my yoke upon you and learn from me, for I am gentle and humble in heart, and you will find rest for your souls. For my yoke is easy and my burden is light.""

Matthew 11:28-30 NIV

It is so good to be able to lean on Jesus, and rest in the security of His Precious Promises!

362.

Bonnie

December

December 1

"For to us a child is born, to us a son is given, and the government will be on his shoulders. And he will be called Wonderful Counselor, Mighty God, Everlasting Father, Prince of Peace. Of the greatness of his government and peace there will be no end. He will reign on David's throne and over his kingdom, establishing and upholding it with justice and righteousness from that time on and forever. The zeal of the Lord Almighty will accomplish this."

Isaiah 9:6-7 NIV

December has arrived, and I am so ready to focus on the Joy of The Birth of Jesus! What a magnificent GIFT!

Bonnie

364.

December 2

"But if we hope for what we do not yet have, we wait for it patiently. In the same way, the Spirit helps us in our weakness. We do not know what we ought to pray for, but the Spirit himself intercedes for us through wordless groans. And he who searches our hearts knows the mind of the Spirit, because the Spirit intercedes for God's people in accordance with the will of God. And we know that in all things God works for the good of those who love him, who have been called according to his purpose."

Romans 8:25-28 NIV

Praying especially today for our missionaries who travel during these difficult times, and who sacrifice much to share the Good News of Christ our Savior!   365.   *Bonnie*

"After Jesus was born in Bethlehem in Judea, during the time of King Herod, Magi from the east came to Jerusalem and asked, "Where is the one who has been born king of the Jews? We saw his star when it rose and have come to worship him." When King Herod heard this he was disturbed, and all Jerusalem with him. When he had called together all the people's chief priests and teachers of the law, he asked them where the Messiah was to be born. "In Bethlehem in Judea," they replied, "for this is what the prophet has written: " 'But you, Bethlehem, in the land of Judah, are by no means least among the rulers of Judah; for out of you will come a ruler who will shepherd my people Israel.'" Then Herod called the Magi secretly and found out from them the exact time the star had appeared. He sent them to Bethlehem and said, "Go and search carefully for the child. As soon as you find him, report to me, so that I too may go and worship him." After they had heard the king, they went on their way, and the star they had seen when it rose went ahead of them until it stopped over the place where the child was. When they saw the star, they were overjoyed. On coming to the house, they saw the child with his mother Mary, and they bowed down and worshiped him. Then they opened their treasures and presented him with gifts of gold, frankincense and myrrh." Matthew 2:1-11 NIV

Do you imagine yourself there, bowing down also, to worship Him?! I do! And what gift would you be bringing to present to Him? I love the song that says "What shall I bring Him? I'll give Him my heart!"

Bonnie

"Rejoice in the Lord always. I will say it again: Rejoice! Let your gentleness be evident to all. The Lord is near. Do not be anxious about anything, but in every situation, by prayer and petition, with thanksgiving, present your requests to God. And the peace of God, which transcends all understanding, will guard your hearts and your minds in Christ Jesus."

Philippians 4:4-7 NIV

These beautiful verses point to the whole reason that each of us has a reason to REJOICE in God's Christmas Gift... it's all about the PEACE that God is willing to provide through the gift of His Only Son JESUS!!

367.

Bonnie

December 5

"Give praise to the Lord, proclaim his name; make known among the nations what he has done. Sing to him, sing praise to him; tell of all his wonderful acts. Glory in his holy name; let the hearts of those who seek the Lord rejoice. Look to the Lord and his strength; seek his face always."

1 Chronicles 16:8-11 NIV

Especially grateful today for those who give of themselves to help spread this Good News "among the nations" of what God has done to provide the way for salvation.

Bonnie

December 6

"But love your enemies, do good to them, and lend to them without expecting to get anything back. Then your reward will be great, and you will be children of the Most High, because he is kind to the ungrateful and wicked. Be merciful, just as your Father is merciful. "Do not judge, and you will not be judged. Do not condemn, and you will not be condemned. Forgive, and you will be forgiven. Give, and it will be given to you. A good measure, pressed down, shaken together and running over, will be poured into your lap. For with the measure you use, it will be measured to you.""

Luke 6:35-38 NIV

Maybe you are making a "Christmas list" and doing a lot of shopping... or maybe you are somewhat depressed because there isn't really enough money in your pocket to buy lavish presents for the ones you love. Maybe your focus needs to change!? Read these verses again with this question in mind: "Are there people I know, who I should seek out to generously offer the "gift of forgiveness"? Try to imagine if your roles were reversed... what would you wish that they would say to you? God will give you the strength to be brave and compassionate... and the result will be a peaceful heart full of JOY!! Money cannot buy that kind of peace and joy!!

Bonnie

"Remember this: Whoever sows sparingly will also reap sparingly, and whoever sows generously will also reap generously. Each of you should give what you have decided in your heart to give, not reluctantly or under compulsion, for God loves a cheerful giver."

2 Corinthians 9:6-7 NIV

Each year about this time, I hear some people talk about NOT enjoying this time of year because they don't feel they can afford to purchase lavish gifts for family and friends. Some don't seem to believe me when I assure them that I do NOT feel that way··· because what we need to focus on is finding some extra ways to simply express our LOVE and FRIENDSHIP, and to LAVISHLY share reminders of GOD'S LOVE, which He demonstrated with a babe in a manger··· coming to be Our Savior!!

Bonnie

December 8

"Now the Lord is the Spirit, and where the Spirit of the Lord is, there is freedom. And we all, who with unveiled faces contemplate the Lord's glory, are being transformed into his image with ever-increasing glory, which comes from the Lord, who is the Spirit."

2 Corinthians 3:17-18 NIV

This is my desire... to be fully "transformed into His image!" This whole chapter... this whole letter to the Corinthians... is amazing!] ... Have a great Sunday worshiping Our Lord!

Bonnie

371.

December 9

"For to us a child is born, to us a son is given, and the government will be on his shoulders. And he will be called Wonderful Counselor, Mighty God, Everlasting Father, Prince of Peace. Of the greatness of his government and peace there will be no end. He will reign on David's throne and over his kingdom, establishing and upholding it with justice and righteousness from that time on and forever. The zeal of the Lord Almighty will accomplish this."

Isaiah 9:6-7 NIV

Especially at Christmas time, we celebrate with joy that Jesus came to bring true Joy and Peace to this world! Let's spread The Word!!

372.

Bonnie

Bonnie's Blessings

"He was despised and rejected by mankind, a man of suffering, and familiar with pain. Like one from whom people hide their faces he was despised, and we held him in low esteem. Surely he took up our pain and bore our suffering, yet we considered him punished by God, stricken by him, and afflicted. But he was pierced for our transgressions, he was crushed for our iniquities; the punishment that brought us peace was on him, and by his wounds we are healed."

Isaiah 53:3-5 NIV

One devotion writer commented: "The prophecy in Isaiah 53 portrays God's great exchange: Jesus' life for all of ours. Jesus knew the cost of Christmas, and He embraced it so we could embrace Him and the eternal life He made available for us. As you celebrate this season, don't forget: we can only be forgiven, healed, and set free because Jesus chose Christmas!"

Bonnie

373.

December 11

"What, then, shall we say in response to these things? If God is for us, who can be against us? He who did not spare his own Son, but gave him up for us all—how will he not also, along with him, graciously give us all things? Who will bring any charge against those whom God has chosen? It is God who justifies. Who then is the one who condemns? No one. Christ Jesus who died—more than that, who was raised to life—is at the right hand of God and is also interceding for us. Who shall separate us from the love of Christ? Shall trouble or hardship or persecution or famine or nakedness or danger or sword? As it is written: "For your sake we face death all day long; we are considered as sheep to be slaughtered." No, in all these things we are more than conquerors through him who loved us. For I am convinced that neither death nor life, neither angels nor demons, neither the present nor the future, nor any powers, neither height nor depth, nor anything else in all creation, will be able to separate us from the love of God that is in Christ Jesus our Lord."

Romans 8:31-39 NIV

My feeble mind simply cannot grasp the magnitude of the message in these verses...literally the Babe In the manger was sent to be my Savior Who died on the cruel cross, then rose again... so that sinners like you and me, could escape hell and have the Gift of Forgiveness and Eternal Life! No gift under your Christmas tree can be greater than the gift that Christ offered when He willingly died on THE TREE!!!

Bonnie

December 12

"And there were shepherds living out in the fields nearby, keeping watch over their flocks at night. An angel of the Lord appeared to them, and the glory of the Lord shone around them, and they were terrified. But the angel said to them, "Do not be afraid. I bring you good news that will cause great joy for all the people. Today in the town of David a Savior has been born to you; he is the Messiah, the Lord.""

Luke 2:8-11 NIV

Believing that these events actually occurred, I sometimes wonder if one of those shepherd boys was amongst the crowds of people who heard the Lord's "Sermon on the Mount", or ate with the multitude of people from one boy's lunch that had been multiplied, and later waved palm branches as Christ made His triumphant entry into Jerusalem; or stood at Calvary's hill staring in horror; but later heard the message on the Day of Pentecost, and then risked everything to share the Good News about the Babe in the Manger, Who now lived in his heart!??!! I truly believe that the "Story of Jesus" is True, and it really happened, and HE gives meaning and purpose and JOY to my life!! How about YOU??!

Bonnie

December 13

"Now may the God of peace, who through the blood of the eternal covenant brought back from the dead our Lord Jesus, that great Shepherd of the sheep, equip you with everything good for doing his will, and may he work in us what is pleasing to him, through Jesus Christ, to whom be glory for ever and ever. Amen."

Hebrews 13:20-21 NIV

This beautiful prayer was included in one of the devotions I was reading this morning. It touched my heart, so I wanted to share it with others. It is my prayer today that each of us would desire to be equipped to only "do what is pleasing to Him"!!

Bonnie

December 14

"For this reason I kneel before the Father, from whom every family in heaven and on earth derives its name. I pray that out of his glorious riches he may strengthen you with power through his Spirit in your inner being, so that Christ may dwell in your hearts through faith. And I pray that you, being rooted and established in love, may have power, together with all the Lord's holy people, to grasp how wide and long and high and deep is the love of Christ, and to know this love that surpasses knowledge—that you may be filled to the measure of all the fullness of God. Now to him who is able to do immeasurably more than all we ask or imagine, according to his power that is at work within us, to him be glory in the church and in Christ Jesus throughout all generations, for ever and ever! Amen."

Ephesians 3:14-21 NIV

This is the Apostle Paul's prayer for the Christians in Ephesus··· but today I would like to lift it up as a prayer for you··· to draw closer to Him this Christmas season, putting HIM before any decorating or gift shopping, or baking goodies.

Bonnie

December 15

"In the sixth month of Elizabeth's pregnancy, God sent the angel Gabriel to Nazareth, a town in Galilee, to a virgin pledged to be married to a man named Joseph, a descendant of David. The virgin's name was Mary. The angel went to her and said, "Greetings, you who are highly favored! The Lord is with you." Mary was greatly troubled at his words and wondered what kind of greeting this might be. But the angel said to her, "Do not be afraid, Mary; you have found favor with God. You will conceive and give birth to a son, and you are to call him Jesus. He will be great and will be called the Son of the Most High. The Lord God will give him the throne of his father David, and he will reign over Jacob's descendants forever; his kingdom will never end." "How will this be," Mary asked the angel, "since I am a virgin?" The angel answered, "The Holy Spirit will come on you, and the power of the Most High will overshadow you. So the holy one to be born will be called the Son of God. Even Elizabeth your relative is going to have a child in her old age, and she who was said to be unable to conceive is in her sixth month. For no word from God will ever fail." "I am the Lord's servant," Mary answered. "May your word to me be fulfilled." Then the angel left her."

Luke 1:26-38 NIV

I believe with all my heart and mind and soul that these events truly occurred. And still I marvel at the faith of those who heard these Words, and responded willingly. My prayer then is that I would respond to His directives, as we read in His Word!!

Bonnie

December 16

"The true light that gives light to everyone was coming into the world. He was in the world, and though the world was made through him, the world did not recognize him. He came to that which was his own, but his own did not receive him. Yet to all who did receive him, to those who believed in his name, he gave the right to become children of God— children born not of natural descent, nor of human decision or a husband's will, but born of God. The Word became flesh and made his dwelling among us. We have seen his glory, the glory of the one and only Son, who came from the Father, full of grace and truth."

John 1:9-14 NIV

This is truly the core of the Christmas blessing: "The Word became flesh and made his dwelling among us." How AMAZING!! Thank You, Lord!

Bonnie

December 17

"Do not be afraid, Mary; you have found favor with God. You will conceive and give birth to a son, and you are to call him Jesus. He will be great and will be called the Son of the Most High. The Lord God will give him the throne of his father David, and he will reign over Jacob's descendants forever; his kingdom will never end.""

Luke 1:30-33 NIV

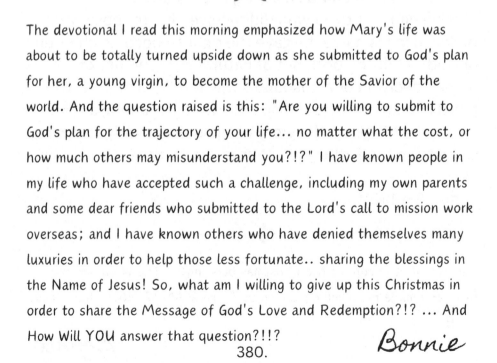

The devotional I read this morning emphasized how Mary's life was about to be totally turned upside down as she submitted to God's plan for her, a young virgin, to become the mother of the Savior of the world. And the question raised is this: "Are you willing to submit to God's plan for the trajectory of your life... no matter what the cost, or how much others may misunderstand you?!?" I have known people in my life who have accepted such a challenge, including my own parents and some dear friends who submitted to the Lord's call to mission work overseas; and I have known others who have denied themselves many luxuries in order to help those less fortunate.. sharing the blessings in the Name of Jesus! So, what am I willing to give up this Christmas in order to share the Message of God's Love and Redemption?!? ... And How Will YOU answer that question?!!?

Bonnie

380.

Bonnie's Blessings

"Therefore if you have any encouragement from being united with Christ, if any comfort from his love, if any common sharing in the Spirit, if any tenderness and compassion, then make my joy complete by being like-minded, having the same love, being one in spirit and of one mind. Do nothing out of selfish ambition or vain conceit. Rather, in humility value others above yourselves, not looking to your own interests but each of you to the interests of the others. In your relationships with one another, have the same mindset as Christ Jesus: Who, being in very nature God, did not consider equality with God something to be used to his own advantage; rather, he made himself nothing by taking the very nature of a servant, being made in human likeness. And being found in appearance as a man, he humbled himself by becoming obedient to death— even death on a cross! Therefore God exalted him to the highest place and gave him the name that is above every name, that at the name of Jesus every knee should bow, in heaven and on earth and under the earth, and every tongue acknowledge that Jesus Christ is Lord, to the glory of God the Father."
Philippians 2:1-11 NIV

Please look over these verses again, as you consider the great sacrifice which Christ made as he came to earth in human form... and not only that... but willingly died on the cruel cross to become the sacrifice which would provide the way for salvation... for you, and for me! The Christmas Gift and the Easter Miracle... all in THE ONE Who came to be our Savior!! Praise Him today by being obedient to His Will in your life!

Bonnie

December 19

"Shout for joy to the Lord, all the earth. Worship the Lord with gladness; come before him with joyful songs. Know that the Lord is God. It is he who made us, and we are his; we are his people, the sheep of his pasture. Enter his gates with thanksgiving and his courts with praise; give thanks to him and praise his name. For the Lord is good and his love endures forever; his faithfulness continues through all generations."

Psalms 100:1-5 NIV

At times it is overwhelming to me, as I try to grasp how immense God's Love is for us······ Think about it! HE loved us (before we were actually born), enough to provide for our need of salvation, by sending Jesus to earth to become our Redeemer!! It really is beyond my comprehension! So the best I can do is to Thank Him, and spend my life striving to obey Him, and tell others this Good News, that The Christ Child was sent to earth to save us!!

Bonnie

December 20

"For to us a child is born, to us a son is given, and the government will be on his shoulders. And he will be called Wonderful Counselor, Mighty God, Everlasting Father, Prince of Peace. Of the greatness of his government and peace there will be no end. He will reign on David's throne and over his kingdom, establishing and upholding it with justice and righteousness from that time on and forever. The zeal of the Lord Almighty will accomplish this."

Isaiah 9:6-7 NIV

Many years before the birth of Jesus, His arrival was prophesied. The Prophet Isaiah penned these beautiful Words. And since there "will be no end" to His greatness, and the peace that He brings... we, therefore, are also blessed!! Praise Him, and celebrate this Good News!!

Bonnie

"But the angel said to them, "Do not be afraid. I bring you good news that will cause great joy for all the people. Today in the town of David a Savior has been born to you; he is the Messiah, the Lord. This will be a sign to you: You will find a baby wrapped in cloths and lying in a manger." Suddenly a great company of the heavenly host appeared with the angel, praising God and saying, "Glory to God in the highest heaven, and on earth peace to those on whom his favor rests." When the angels had left them and gone into heaven, the shepherds said to one another, "Let's go to Bethlehem and see this thing that has happened, which the Lord has told us about.""

Luke 2:10-15 NIV

When Bud and I were privileged to make a trip to The Holy Land with a group many years ago, tourists were not allowed to go to Bethlehem, due to some civil unrest that was happening, so that was a disappointment at the time. Still, it is awesome to picture in our minds that precious scene many years prior... The Son of God... resting in a bed of hay. Thank You, Lord for this Amazing Gift of Love!

Bonnie

December 22

"For there is born to you this day in the city of David a Savior, who is Christ the Lord. And this will be the sign to you: You will find a Babe wrapped in swaddling cloths, lying in a manger." And suddenly there was with the angel a multitude of the heavenly host praising God and saying: "Glory to God in the highest, And on earth peace, goodwill toward men!" So it was, when the angels had gone away from them into heaven, that the shepherds said to one another, "Let us now go to Bethlehem and see this thing that has come to pass, which the Lord has made known to us.""

Luke 2:11-15 NKJV

Do you have some favorite passages in the Bible that spark your imagination? This is one of them for me! Surely it was overwhelming and magnificent! And an event that would come to mind every day for the rest of your lifetime... especially if I had been amongst the shepherds who hurried to visit the family in the stable, and adored the precious baby in the manger!! Oh Lord, help me to always be in awe of this miraculous event!

Bonnie

385.

December 23

"Let your light so shine before men, that they may see your good works and glorify your Father in heaven."

Matthew 5:16 NKJV

This verse can carry a sweet thought as we share the Joy of Christmas with others: even more than the lovely lights on the Christmas tree, let's let the light of Christ's love shine from us to everyone we come in contact with this season!! Let HIM shine through YOU ... to everyone you meet!! ... and let it begin in your own home and family!

Bonnie

December 24

"For to us a child is born, to us a son is given, and the government will be on his shoulders. And he will be called Wonderful Counselor, Mighty God, Everlasting Father, Prince of Peace. Of the greatness of his government and peace there will be no end. He will reign on David's throne and over his kingdom, establishing and upholding it with justice and righteousness from that time on and forever. The zeal of the Lord Almighty will accomplish this."

Isaiah 9:6-7 NIV

When we pause to consider that some of the prophecies about the birth of the Christ Child were literally penned centuries before Mary laid her baby in a manger .... it is then we are reminded that God had a magnificent sacrificial plan... and He did it because He Loved You and Me, BEFORE we each even took our first breath!!! The God Who created the whole universe KNOWS YOU BY NAME.... and HE LOVES YOU THAT MUCH!!!

Bonnie

December 24

"But the angel said to them, "Do not be afraid. I bring you good news that will cause great joy for all the people. Today in the town of David a Savior has been born to you; he is the Messiah, the Lord. This will be a sign to you: You will find a baby wrapped in cloths and lying in a manger." Suddenly a great company of the heavenly host appeared with the angel, praising God and saying, "Glory to God in the highest heaven, and on earth peace to those on whom his favor rests.""

Luke 2:10-14 NIV

The devotional thought in today's reading points out from these verses that the angels could have pointed out so very many attributes of the Christ-child but they focus at that moment PEACE!.... Prayer: Lord, we each need Your Peace in our hearts, just to make it thru each day! But perhaps even more so, this WORLD needs to acknowledge and accept the True Peace which can only come from YOU!

Bonnie

December 25

"When the angels had left them and gone into heaven, the shepherds said to one another, "Let's go to Bethlehem and see this thing that has happened, which the Lord has told us about." So they hurried off and found Mary and Joseph, and the baby, who was lying in the manger. When they had seen him, they spread the word concerning what had been told them about this child, and all who heard it were amazed at what the shepherds said to them. But Mary treasured up all these things and pondered them in her heart. The shepherds returned, glorifying and praising God for all the things they had heard and seen, which were just as they had been told."

Luke 2:15-20 NIV.

As we celebrate Christmas this year, may we each search our own hearts and ask what we are personally doing to share the Love of Jesus with those closest to us... as well as spreading the Good News around the world! What does true Peace look like in Your Home and Your Heart this Christmas?

Merry Christmas!   389.   *Bonnie*

"You will keep in perfect peace those whose minds are steadfast, because they trust in you. Trust in the Lord forever, for the Lord, the Lord himself, is the Rock eternal."

Isaiah 26:3-4 NIV

Indeed this is the hope of Christmas... Peace on Earth, goodwill toward men... Surely we all long for perfect peace... both in our hearts and in the world at large! And this is what Christ came to earth to deliver to us: "Peace on Earth, Goodwill to men." Let's pray that such peace can reside in our hearts and that we can share that Good News with others by what we say and do in the coming year.

Bonnie

December 27

"Dear friends, let us love one another, for love comes from God. Everyone who loves has been born of God and knows God. Whoever does not love does not know God, because God is love. This is how God showed his love among us: He sent his one and only Son into the world that we might live through him. This is love: not that we loved God, but that he loved us and sent his Son as an atoning sacrifice for our sins. Dear friends, since God so loved us, we also ought to love one another. No one has ever seen God; but if we love one another, God lives in us and his love is made complete in us."

1 John 4:7-12 NIV

It seems to me that these verses describe to true essence of Christmas! Let's display and share His Love throughout the year ahead!

Bonnie

December 28

So, friends, we can now—without hesitation—walk right up to God, into "the Holy Place." Jesus has cleared the way by the blood of his sacrifice, acting as our priest before God. The "curtain" into God's presence is his body. So let's do it —full of belief, confident that we're presentable inside and out. Let's keep a firm grip on the promises that keep us going. He always keeps his word. Let's see how inventive we can be in encouraging love and helping out, not avoiding worshiping together as some do but spurring each other on, especially as we see the big Day approaching."

Hebrews 10:19-25 MSG

As we approach a new year on the calendar, let's agree to "Spur each other on" with words of encouragement, and with acts of kindness! And with more time in His Word daily!

Bonnie

December 29

"Do nothing out of selfish ambition or vain conceit. Rather, in humility value others above yourselves, not looking to your own interests but each of you to the interests of the others."

Philippians 2:3-4 NIV

This is pretty basic advice on how to live a Christ-like life. Be considerate of the needs of others, more than your own.

393.

Bonnie

December 30

"We who are strong ought to bear with the failings of the weak and not to please ourselves."

Romans 15:1 NIV

There is definitely a message here for every one of us, at some point in our lives. Praise God for His great Love and Care. Lean on HIM today!

Bonnie

Bonnie's Blessings

"Finally, brothers and sisters, whatever is true, whatever is noble, whatever is right, whatever is pure, whatever is lovely, whatever is admirable—if anything is excellent or praiseworthy—think about such things."

Philippians 4:8 NIV

Wholesome Words to close out this year.... and looking forward to such an admirable goal for the new year! May the Lord guide you and Bless you as you bring everything to His Throne Room, and "think about such things!"

Bonnie

395.

May the Lord bless you and keep you,

Bonnie

Made in the USA
Monee, IL
12 February 2024

53392625R00223